Can't Doesn't Exist

Why cancer can't beat me, and you
can be anything that you want to be

Joshua M.
Gordon

David M.
Prentice

DEDICATION

To Glenn Prentice, for teaching Dave that Can't Doesn't
Exist.

ACKNOWLEDGMENTS

From Dave: Unfortunately, with the change of the publication date, Dave wasn't able to communicate what he wanted to be in the acknowledgments section. Hopefully, in a future re-print/edit, we will be able to update this with his thoughts. For right now, I'll tell you this...

I know he is incredibly grateful to his entire family. He spent the duration of our interviews doing nothing but talking positive about everybody. Caren, he appreciates you more than he knows how to show, and loves you with all his heart. I'd name every family member individually, but truly, just know that he loves and appreciates each and every one of you, and he put effort into making that very, very clear. To the family that were specifically discussed in this book, please know that he saw everything that 'wasn't perfect' as just part of life, and was appreciative of all that you have done for him. He spent a great deal of time speaking very highly of you all, and it was clear to me that you guys are of utmost importance to him.

From Josh: My family, for understanding the ridiculous change in my schedule that this mission demanded. Your support is amazing, and the only reason I can do what I do. Thank you for always working to make the world better, and inspiring me to try to keep up with you. And to all the people who have helped get Dave's story and message out to the world, I thank you from the bottom of my heart. His message can change the world, and if it weren't for you guys, it might never have gotten out there.

David M. Prentice and Joshua M. Gordon

Table of Contents

9/16/2020

What this was...

In the beginning, this was a mission. Not a simple one, but a mission none-the-less. The goal was to help people. We wanted them to be happy, we wanted them to be wealthy, we wanted them to be free.

I'll explain who 'we' is in just a little bit.

What this now is...

Now, this is a tragedy. It's also a victory. And a loss, and a win. "Can't Doesn't Exist" is an exploration of what turned David Prentice into one of the most amazing men to ever walk the Earth; a man I'm honored to consider a brother.

September of 2020, our original plans for this book were thrown out the window. In what seemed like the blink of an eye, everything changed.

And it wasn't just our plans that changed. No, in fact, almost everything changed; even the title. The original title was going to be a carefully chosen set of words, all designed with the goal of helping inform and intrigue the potential reader. We tossed around ideas like 'How to win, no matter what', and 'They're all wrong, you can be great', but, once September came, those ideas went right out the window. Push had come to shove, and there was no choice; "Can't Doesn't Exist" was the only name this book could be given, because Can't Doesn't Exist is the phrase that has defined the life of David Prentice. From homelessness to millionaire, from a hundred pounds over-weight to six-pack abs, from high school dropout to successful business owner, "Can't Doesn't Exist" just describes David Prentice far too well for this book to possibly be named anything else.

And, just as a side note, if you want to change your life in ways you've likely never imagined, start out by implementing that thought. *Can't doesn't exist*...if you can understand that, you are going to be in for an amazing, wild, and wonderful ride in this life.

Now, what is this book? Let me start with what it isn't. The original plan was to write two books. One was to be a human interest story, and the other was going to be a success book. We outlined both, and then wrote the human interest story first.

The original manuscript was completed in early August of 2020, and by mid-August we were beginning to get the promotional materials together. Then, everything went to crap.

In the next chapter, I'm going to tell you all about what was going on. Then, once you know where things are, we will jump into the original manuscript, with some modifications, of which I will note when you get there.

For right now, know this:

Life is meant to be lived, no matter what.

For a long time, I thought I knew that. I thought I understood that. And, at a cursory glance, I did. But, this experience has taught me how important it is to not just know that, to not just understand that, but to live that. Dave's life has given me that; for which I'm forever indebted. If you feel as though you understand that, I challenge you to take moment and evaluate if you actually live that. If you find that the answer is no, then start doing it right now. Live life, no matter your circumstances.

Now, what we are about to talk about, is an amazing story. A story of a man who doesn't know how to quit. A story of a man that fights, to the end, no matter what. A man who can take a punch, and keep going. A man that in certain ways, we should all strive to be like.

His story is wild, and if you are anything like me, it will leave you laughing, crying, and awestruck, but, please know that entertainment is not our goal. If this is merely entertainment, we have failed. While both David and I hope you enjoy the book, our deepest desire is that as you read this, it helps you improve your life.

Alright, it's time to get to the good stuff. Turn the page, and let me tell you about the crazy journey that has been David Prentice's life.

David M. Prentice and Joshua M. Gordon

NEXT THING WE KNOW

I hate to do this, but I have to give away the whole story, right at the start. While that doesn't make for very good story telling, it's the only way this is going to make sense.

So, in the name of necessity, here's the short version of David's story.

Crazy childhood, crazy teen years. David overcomes gigantic volumes of adversity, and ends up living what he calls a 'dream life'.

At 28, David has a seizure on Father's Day. After going to the hospital and undergoing the appropriate testing, he finds out he has a grade 2 Astrocytoma; brain cancer.

They do surgery, cut out a bunch of the tumor, and he loses his ability to use his right side properly. Most of the things that we take for granted, he has to learn how to do all over again. He has to learn how to walk. He has to learn how to tie his shoes. He has to learn how to write, and type, and even to speak. So, to be clear, while I already stated that this man knows adversity, I feel it is necessary to point out that he not only knows it, but knows adversity in ways that most of us never will.

Here's the thing though, David Prentice is a crazy man. A fighter. A man who doesn't know how to quit. In the face of the immense struggles that brain cancer and brain surgery brought, David fights, and learns how to do everything he couldn't do, and ends up with one of the most amazing recovery stories you will ever hear (of which I will tell you all about in the coming chapters).

Then, after having an amazing recovery, he and his 'dream wife' to compliment his 'dream life' (all his words), take an amazing 40 day trip to Europe and Africa, where, sadly, he has another seizure (actually, many), and is forced to cancel the trip early and come home for emergency medical care.

Another brain surgery occurs, along with a horrifying diagnosis that he may be dead in as little as three weeks. That was January of 2020. As of the day of this writing, September 16, 2020, Dave is still alive and fighting.

After the second surgery, David could walk, but barely. The function on his right side was so damaged that while he could walk, it was in a broken, painful fashion. By June, David was ready to start working on fixing his body, and he began to re-learn how to walk, now for the second time.

One month in, David was walking properly and pain free. He could go up and down the stairs with no issue, and his recovery was once again blowing the minds of all who were involved; particularly mine.

Only for the sake of introduction and clarity, I'm Josh, and I'm Dave's trainer.

Once Dave was able to walk again, he wasted no time in asking if he could run.

"No," I replied.

"Why not?" he asked.

"Because you just learned how to walk, and the fall risk is gigantic. It's too dangerous. Not yet," I said.

Well, I fought him on it, but he fought harder, and we

agreed that we would attempt teaching him how to run again.

Sure as can be, as Dave is patterned to do, one month later, he was running. It was astounding. Here is this guy, barely able to go up a flight of stairs, and in two months, he's running. Then he asked me about running a 5k that was set to take place only six weeks later on October 4th.

Like I said, he's crazy.

"No," I told him.

"Why not?" he asked, in a comical repetition of our 'can I run' conversation.

"Because right now you can run 200 feet. That's a long way from running a 5k."

"Yeah," he replied, "but two months ago I couldn't walk, and you fixed that. One month ago I couldn't run, and we fixed that too. So you're going to have to explain to me why I can't run the 5k when we have a full six weeks to prepare for it."

I spent the next five minutes explaining to Dave how while we had trained him to run, he was only capable of running at a certain speed, and to run three plus miles would require him to be able to modulate his speed up and down, which was something that, at least at that point in time, he wasn't able to do.

"Then you'll teach me," he replied.

We talked, and, as usual, he fought for the ability to fight. I told him he was crazy, and he just smiled and lifted his brows. Knowing him well enough, I can confidently tell you that this was simply his way of saying he knew it was a crazy goal, and he didn't care.

Eventually, he convinced me to let him try.

We tried, and he was crushing it. Every session he was getting more and more distance in. What started with a few 100 feet, turned into a half a mile in what seemed like no time. Just two weeks into it, he was able to run 10 minutes straight for the first time since the brain surgery, covering over a mile in that time. And that's the craziest part; he wasn't just running, he was running faster than most people ever will.

The 5k David wanted to run is a fundraiser for brain cancer research, and he had run it both last year and the year before. It didn't matter if he had just re-learned to walk a few months prior, this race mattered too much for him to not give everything he had to make it happen. After the insane success he was having, I realized that what he wanted was actually possible, despite my initial reservations.

"You know what Dave, you'll be able to do this," I said, astounded that I had actually said those words.

"Of course I will," he replied, as though it was a given.

Dave's body was recovering at an astounding rate, and everybody was excited. Knowing how great a story it was, we decided to start filming some of it and posted it online with the hashtag #watchdavewin. We got three videos in, and everything was going great. People were replying, getting inspired, and we were making the world better while we made Dave better. Which made us both all sorts of happy.

And then, things changed.

Dave was on a myriad of medications, and the doctors he has been working with (who are fabulous by the way) were trying to get the best balance possible, which meant reducing the volume of steroids that David was on. After the seizures, the brain surgeries, and the brain cancer, David's brain had a ton of inflammation, and the steroids were being used to control that inflammation. But, there are problems that come with the steroids, and the team was trying to get Dave on as low a dose as he could properly function with. The hope was that he could progressively wean off of them completely, if possible.

As his medications were being changed, you could see that he was feeling the effects. Despite having been through six plus rounds of chemo, this was the first time I ever heard him say he felt 'crappy'. Beyond feeling poor, he was struggling in ways that he hadn't in months. His right hand was losing function. His right foot would occasionally fail to lift properly. There was trouble, but we didn't know from what. Was it the tumor growing back? Was it the medication changes? We didn't know, but something was wrong, and that was obvious.

September 14, 2020, Dave had an MRI to see what was going on. It was the news none of us wanted. The tumor had grown, spiderwebbing through his brain, making a third surgery unlikely to be of use. And in just one small moment, the entire story changed. The doctors said he might have only a few months left. He's still fighting, but we are officially at the point of needing a miracle.

And that brings us to what you are about to read. As I mentioned, what follows this section is the original book, with a few changes. Where this book was originally about success, it is now about something far more important...

Life, and living it, while we have it.

There's just one more thing I need to say before you get started. This book, is a lot like life. It's not perfect. We were in the process of editing when everything went awry with David's health, and it was at that point that I made the executive decision that done was better than perfect (thanks Chandler Bolt).

I can tell you right now that there are two separate parts where I feel the book is a bit repetitive. It has remained that way, and not been changed, because every test reader we used vehemently disagreed with me. They said that while the topics were similar, they were taught from different views, and helped them. We decided that if it helped them, we would keep the book just the way it was. Also, because of the need to get this out so quickly, there were rounds of editing that while we normally would have gone through, we just couldn't; not under the time constraints that is. That means that there's probably a semicolon where there should be a comma, and vice versa. Hopefully, that's about it. Either way, what that means, is that as you read, I have to ask that you will give us some grace, and look at this book like life; imperfect, and that's okay.

As for Dave, he just wants to do everything he can to change the world. He wanted to write this book to help make *your* life better. And, in light of his current condition, and the unknown state of his longevity, I felt the need was there to get this book out immediately so that he could see it, hold it, and see what it does for people.

In this book, you're going to learn about the success principles that Dave used not just to become a millionaire before he was 30, but also to live an amazing life that was both fulfilling, and world changing. We will breakdown each rule, ensuring that you know exactly how to implement them in your life. Then, after the parts of the book where you will learn what to do, and how to do it, you will find a series of challenges that we are calling 'Dave's Challenge #X'. The truth is, these challenges aren't really a challenge from Dave to you, but in fact, an opportunity for *you* to challenge yourself. If you take the challenges, we are both confident that you will find what you need in order to live a happier life, and to improve not just *your* world, but *the* world. If you choose to implement these principles, you will be choosing to improve your life, and if you do so, we want to hear about it. Whether you are just starting out, or have already found a success, help Dave and I out by letting us know. You can do so by posting something to social media with the hashtag #watchdavewin. We'll be watching it, and would love to hear about the challenges that you've overcome; it'll mean the world to both of us. Speaking of the world, that's the other awesome thing about you sharing your successes. When you put that post up, about your challenge and your success, you are going to help the world. *You* are going to challenge the world. *You* are going to make a difference, and I thank you for it.

Just as a reminder, everything from the beginning of the next chapter, until the end note, was put together while everything was going great. When this was written, it looked like things were working out the way everybody hopes they would work out. Keep that in mind as you read.

Now, for the wild ride that is David Prentice's life…

David M. Prentice and Joshua M. Gordon

(The original introduction)

A note for the reader...
(read this, or you will be confused)

What you are about to read, is a crazy compilation of the story of David Prentice, his rise from poverty to success, his fight with cancer, and the lessons he wants you to know so that you can have a better life, now. Dave has been told he will likely be dead any day now, and he has decided that he has no intent of dying without first doing everything he can to make the world a better place. This book is part of his attempt at doing so.

As you read, I'm confident that you will notice there are two distinct types of content in this book. This odd combination of information, is the result of Dave's two goals, which I give to you in no particular order.

1 - Dave wants to teach people how to go from poverty to millionaire, just like he did.

2 - The strategies he's used as a cancer survivor to not just avoid death, but to survive, and thrive.

You're likely thinking that those two things make for quite an odd combination. If it means anything, I agree. And, when Dave approached me about writing this book, I didn't think it could work. But, as we explored the idea, something great happened. He made something clear to me, that until he told me, I simply didn't know.

It turns out, the same rules he used to become a millionaire before he was thirty, are the same rules he's used to thrive through a brain cancer diagnosis that he was told would have him dead back in January of 2020, and because of that, it actually made sense that they might be taught together.

Beyond knowing how weird a combination it sounds like, I also know that some of you, will simply not be interested in certain parts. Some people just want to hear about the guy who had his head cut open, was paralyzed, and can walk again. It's a great story, and I wanted to hear it just as badly as anybody else, so I get it. For that person, you might not be interested in the portions on business success, goal setting, controlling your influences, or any of the rules David has used to succeed; and that's okay. But, let me make a suggestion. Even if you think that content isn't for you, don't skip it. You'll be missing out. Likewise, if you only care about becoming some big real estate investor, and that's how you know about Dave, and don't care at all about his backstory, or his cancer, I understand why you might want to skip those sections, but, I assure you, if you skip them, you'll be missing out.

Like most of life, this book is yours to do with as you wish. If you want to skip, you can, but, just like life, if you skip stuff, you will never know what you have lost. I beg of you, don't miss out.

IT'S OUR JOB

"Okay, so, what's this all about?" I asked, curious to see if this was anything more than just business.

"People," he replied.

"People?"

"Yeah. I want to help people," he said.

"Who?" I asked.

"All of them."

"But, who is 'all of them'?"

"All of them is every and any person that I can help," he said. "Listen, I'm going to die one day, and if I'm going to die, I'm not going out without doing something that matters."

"I get that," I replied, "that makes sense. Is that why we are here?"

"Indeed," he said. "We are here for one reason and one reason alone; to do something that matters."

Knowing our goal was to help people was refreshing. Money is nice, but helping people is better; it was good to see that our goals lined up.

"Also," he said, "and yeah, I already know that this will destroy downloads of *(title of success book)*, but at some point in this book we need to make sure we have gone through all the rules."

NOTE TO THE READER: Originally, the 'success principles' book was going to be released before this one. By the time this book would have been finished, the success book would have been titled and corrected here, but, alas.

"You want to go through all of the rules?" I asked.

"Yeah, all of them."

"Well, it's your book. If you aren't worried about it, I'm not worried about it."

"Alright, good," he said. "Besides, those who are going to get *(insert title here)*, are going to buy it, and those who aren't, aren't. That's okay. If they want to do it, they can, but let's make sure that anybody that reads this book knows the rules."

"Want to make a table?" I asked.

"No, too simple," he said. "It would be a good way to sell the other book, but let's really give them what they need to be able to put the rules to use."

"Okay, full explanations. Got it."

"Good," he replied, "because if people really want to change their lives, we might as well show them how!"

"I like it," I said, pausing to take a bite of an unusually peppery piece of beef jerky.

"The jerky?" he asked.

"No, the idea," I replied, laughing. "I mean, yes, I like the jerky too, but I was talking about the idea of helping people."

"I figured," he said, "that's why you are here."

The here being referred to, was the very much under construction home of David Prentice; the man whom I thought was going to be the focus of this book.

While David can live practically anywhere he wants, it is the city of Detroit that he chooses to call home. To no surprise to anybody who knows him, and irrelevant to the multitude of housing options he has, David chose not to buy a finished home that he could just move into and enjoy. Instead, he bought a house that would require a full-scale remodel, because that's how he tends to operate. He found a beautiful home that was built in 1927, which, to put it lightly, had seen far better days. David and his wife Caren bought the home in 2018, and as soon as the city would let them, they poured their blood, sweat, tears, and money, into making it into something beautiful. Where everybody else saw a beat down home, Dave saw potential.

At the time of our first interview, the construction was almost finished. Most of the plaster had been done. The trim work was near complete, and the kitchen was in, and beautiful. Sure, the main floor bathroom had no door, and yes, you could definitely step on a nail if you weren't careful, but the finish line was close.

♦♦♦

"Wait," I said, stopping to clarify what he meant. "I'm here because I like the idea, or, to help people?"

"Both," he replied. "You are here because I want to help people, and I knew you would like the idea. Besides, it's our job. You and me; we're supposed to do things like this. Think about it. I've figured it out. You've figured it out. You're the guy that wrote the book on happiness, and I'm the guy who wrote the book on success. If anybody is going to be able to help people improve their lives, it's us."

That made sense, but it didn't mean we should do it.

"Okay, I like that," I replied. "Next step is to dial in on who the reader is."

"Everybody," Dave replied, in his characteristically optimistic type of way.

"I wish, but it won't be everybody. It's too broad. We can help everybody who reads the book, but some people just won't do it. Some people don't read. We have to ask the question of who it is that will actually sit down, and read this book."

"Well, with my name on it, it will likely be real estate people or cancer people," he replied.

"Good. You've got influence in real estate, and an amazing story in regards to the cancer part of life, so those make sense. But they're not just kind of unrelated, they're completely unrelated. We might have to pick one."

"No," Dave replied. "People in real estate think big picture. At least, successful people in real estate think big picture. Those people are going to get that the things that impact life, also impact business, and they'll want to read it for that reason. The rookie who can't think big might not, but that's okay, we can't make everybody happy and I'm fine with that. And the story itself, well, that's broad, so it covers nearly everybody anyways. I mean, it sucks, but who doesn't have someone in their life that has to deal with cancer? It's a shame; it's just too freaking common man, and that means that almost anybody can relate there."

"And you think we can somehow, in some way, write a book to both markets? One book, not two?" I asked.

"I do," he replied. "If we spend enough time brainstorming, we'll figure it out. We always do."

"Alright, I'll bite. Let's explore it. If we are going to write to both markets, you have to tell me what sets you apart? There's a whole lot of real estate investors out there. And, not to be so insensitive, but there are a whole lot of cancer survivors out there too. What's different about you? How will your advice actually help the reader? If we are going to be able to put a book together to help people, we have to be able to explain to them why they should even listen?"

Dave and I have been friends for a long time, so, when Dave looked at me like I was an idiot, the comical look on his face failed to give me an answer, but succeeded greatly at getting me to laugh. Thankfully, he did in fact have a good answer.

"For one thing," he replied, "there aren't a 'whole lot of' real estate investors out there like me. Most of them work insane hours, and lose their mind working their tail off. 99% of them hate their lives. My life, however, is amazing. I work when I want to. I work with who I want to. And while there was a point that I had to work hard, that's in the past. I certainly don't have to anymore. Also, there might be a lot of people in real estate, but, Josh, I'll tell you, they aren't like me."

"Okay," I replied, "but what about the cancer end? Maybe you're unique in the real estate world, but the cancer world? There's got to be something near ten bazillion books out there on cancer. You're going to have to have something more than 'eat more veggies' if we are actually going to help people."

"No kidding," he replied, still looking at me like I hadn't figured it out.

"So, what are you going to give them? How are you going to help your fellow cancer patients?"

"Survivors," he replied, forcefully.

"Survivors?" I asked, confused by the difference.

"Yeah, I can't help people that want to be cancer patients. I can only help cancer patients that want to be cancer survivors," he said.

♦♦♦

I knew exactly where Dave was going. He's got a mindset. It's a simple one, and it goes like this:

"Win."

It's that simple, 'win'. I wouldn't say he's interested in winning at all costs, but if he's going to play, he plans on winning.

The more time I've spent with Dave, the more I've discovered that this 'win' mindset is not just about sports or business. In fact, the 'win' mindset plays into every moment of David's life.

Six months prior to our first interview, David was told he had as little as three weeks left to live. He was diagnosed with a rapidly growing grade four glioblastoma, a rare and deadly form of brain cancer. He has survived it, and he credits his survival to a combination of factors, including great medical care, great family support, and more, but there was a lynch pin in the process that he credits his success to. That lynch pin, that 'secret sauce', is the idea that when you do anything, you do it to win.

♦♦♦

As we were sitting, I noticed a stack of bills sitting several inches high on the table. He was remodeling a home; they could easily have been contractor bills. He was also in the midst of half a million dollars plus in medical bills due to his two brain surgeries, chemo treatments, radiation, etc., etc., etc. Which stack of bills it was, I don't know.

"Then, are we not trying to help cancer patients? Just cancer *survivors*?" I asked.

"No. We are trying to *make* cancer patients, *into* cancer survivors."

Dave started to shift around in his chair. It was as though all of the energy in his body wanted to get out, and it couldn't get out fast enough through his mouth, forcing him to move around like a small child who needed to use the bathroom. If it was easier for him, I imagine he would have stood up and marched around the room as he spoke.

"Listen," he began, "people need to know what matters. Outlook, matters. Mindset, matters. Will; that's what matters. These people who are in this battle, some of them don't know how to fight. We are going to teach them how to fight, and in doing so, we are going to make patients into survivors. Get it?"

"I do. But tell me, how do we do that?"

♦♦♦

Dave's going to answer that question, but not right here; we will get to it later in the book.

Everything you've read so far, was all part of our planning session. We had sat down with the intent to establish things like the goals of the book, deadlines, the mission, etc., but, as is usual when Dave and I talk, our conversation had snowballed out of control, and we had delved deeper into his story than we were supposed to.

Despite knowing what the goal was, we still needed to know (other than writing a book), exactly how Dave wanted to help people. He had already written a book about getting wealthy, so what was this one going to be about? Cancer survival, life management, another one on wealth? That was the question we needed to figure out.

♦♦♦

"Where do you want to start?" I asked.

"Do I get to choose?" he asked.

"I think so. After all, it is your book."

"Yeah, but you're the writer, so, isn't that your department?" he replied, lifting his chin in a particularly 'David' type of way.

◆◆◆

As you will soon come to see, David Prentice's life story is insane. Despite a pile of challenges, and the means to live a life of luxury, all he really wants to do is help people.

Dave's been told he won't live forever, and his biggest concern is that he doesn't die without having helped people in some way that matters. He was already philanthropic, and he had already done the mentor thing, but, he wanted more. Specifically, he wanted to 'scale up' his ability to help, and this book was step one.

When he first contacted me about this, the original idea was to ghostwrite for him. We did it with his success book, and both of us were very happy with the end result. The thing about Dave is that while he's got a great story that could truly help people, he's in no position to write a book by himself; particularly because at the time of this writing, he couldn't use his right hand.

"Instead of ghostwriting, have you thought about just dictating?" I asked.

"I did," he replied, "but let's be real, books and speaking are two different things. Great writers write, great speakers speak. Sometimes people are both, and sometimes they aren't. I'd rather let you clean up my ugly grammar and crappy vocabulary, than me do it by myself and have a lesser product. We are better together, let's just do it that way."

I didn't disagree, and here we are.

David's inability to use his right hand is one of the side effects of his most recent brain surgery. He's gone under the knife twice now, with each brain surgery creating its own challenges. The first one mostly impacted his right leg, and the second one spread beyond it, leaving him with a very low level of function on his entire right side.

Something most people don't know, is that we have far more than just the five primary senses. Beyond sight, smell, taste, etc., we also have a very valuable, and very specific, sense of pressure. When we touch something, pressure is an integral part of knowing what is happening, and without it, fine motor skills are near impossible. Unfortunately, after the second surgery, Dave's sense of pressure was greatly damaged. That damage means that at the time of this book's inception, he lacked the fine motor control necessary to type out a book.

David was a willing and dedicated rehab patient, but any progress he was going to make was drastically hindered by the challenges that COVID-19 brought. While David did not come down with the virus itself, access to therapy was slowed down drastically as the entire world attempted to figure out how to mix things like in-person therapies, with a pandemic that was ravaging the entire world. Oh, and don't forget, David lives in the city of Detroit, Michigan.

When COVID-19 began attacking the United States, Detroit was one of the worst 'hotspots' in the entire country, and everything, including therapies, was drastically slowed down. All of that is to say that David typing out a memoir, or a book on real estate success, or cancer survival, or, even an email, wasn't going to be happening any time soon. And that's where I came in.

Obviously, I'm rewinding a bit here, but just to fill you in, so please pardon my break in chronology. Our first conversation about the book started with whether or not I would be interested, and quickly jumped to if it would work.

♦♦♦

"Dave, what are you an expert in?" I asked, hoping to answer my conundrum of what this book was supposed to be about.

Dave took no time to think, responding near instantly.

"Winning," he replied.

"Then that's what the book is about," I said, quite happy with his answer.

"Winning?" he asked.

"Yes, winning. Winning helps cancer patients, --" oh, man. I stopped myself in my tracks, realizing I had called them patients instead of survivors, knowing all too well that Dave was going to take issue with that one.

"Survivors," he said, in a forceful but friendly manner.

"Yes," I replied, "I agree. Survivors."

"And the investors?" he asked.

"Winning helps investors too," I replied. "Winning helps everybody. So, if we are trying to 'scale up' helping people, that's what we do, we teach them how to win."

DREAMS END

Let me step back for a second, and fill you in a little bit. My name is Joshua Gordon, and as far as this book is concerned, I don't matter. David would tell you otherwise, but that's just because he's secretly a really nice guy, and cares about me as a friend.

The man you will be hearing about, the man I am interviewing, is David Prentice, a 30 year old real estate investor who's had more than his share of ups and downs. While David has made it to the status of millionaire before even arriving at the age of 30, he is anything but an overnight success. Nor did he come from money. From living in a trailer, to homelessness, David was born with anything but a silver spoon in his mouth. In fact, he might not have even had a spoon, yet alone a silver one.

For David, it was hard work, that was eventually complimented by smart work, that allowed him to build his business into the giant that it is now.

Having failed his way to what he calls 'freedom', David has built up a successful real estate firm, found financial success, and met and married the love of his life. If this were March of 2018, and you were to ask him what he thought of his life, he would have told you it was a dream.

Unfortunately, dreams end.

Father's Day 2018, David suffered a grand mal seizure;

the first, of multiple.

A short ambulance ride to a nearby hospital was followed by a diagnosis of a seven plus centimeter brain tumor; the product of brain cancer. David's dream life, was being turned into a nightmare.

Now, dear reader, do me a favor. Take a second, and imagine that. One moment you are cleaning dishes, and the next, you are finding out you have a baseball sized tumor inside your skull. I don't care how tough you are, how worldly you are, or how downright grizzled you are; that's rough.

◆◆◆

"What was it like?" I asked
"Annoying."
"That's it? Annoying?"
"Yeah. I was 28 years old. I had everything. This was crap, and I wasn't okay with it. So, yeah, annoying."

"Were you scared?"
"No. I didn't think I was going to die. I don't do that. I win," he replied, predictably.
"There are things other than death though? What about chemo, radiation, surgeries, all of that? Surely you were scared of that," I replied.
"I might have been," he said. "Somewhere deep inside, in a place I don't know. In that place, yeah, maybe chemo and all of that might have been scary; but it's nowhere I'm really aware of. You got to understand, I'm dumb like that. I'm not interested in honest evaluation; I'm interested in victory. Being scared would only slow me down, so even if there was some deep hidden part of me that had me wetting myself, I don't know that I would even recognize it."

"What about the cost?" I asked. "Did that weigh in on you?"

"Sure, that's why I wanted to leave the hospital," he replied.

"Leave?"

"Yeah, when I first got there, I felt fine. I told them I was okay, and that I wanted to go home, but they were having none of that."

"You had a seizure and passed out, didn't you think you probably needed to stay and get things looked at?"

"No," he replied. "I was just thinking holy crap I don't feel like spending tens of thousands of dollars on unneeded tests."

"But they convinced you to stay."

"Yeah, thankfully," he replied. "I might be dumb sometimes, but I'm not so dumb as to not listen to people who know better than I do."

"Like oncologists and neurosurgeons," I replied.

"Exactly."

One of David's dogs, Onyx, a ridiculously large Great Dane that makes David's wife look like a small child, came over to me and stared at me for a moment. Onyx was used to seeing me standing, where his head only comes up to my chest. With me seated, this big beautiful 200lb pile of gray, had his head at the same height as mine, and seemed confused. It may have been the moment he realized he was bigger than me. It may have been that he smelled the beef jerky on my breath and wondered how he gets some. I don't know.

He knows his position in the pack well-enough though, and Onyx lowered his head as he attempted to recruit some affection. I gave him a quick head rub and attempted to send him off. I was at best 10 percent successful, but a quick word from Dave, and Onyx headed out of the room to go lay on the couch. "Not a bad life," I thought. Maybe an uneventful one, but probably not a bad one.

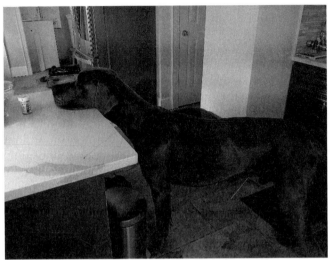

No, that's not a small horse…that's Onyx

"So you listened to them, and stayed."

"For several weeks," he replied, "which sucked."

"Tell me about it."

"You were there," he said, laughing.

"I know, but I want to know what it was like from your perspective, not mine."

I was there, but not anywhere as much as Dave gives me credit for.

Dave and I have had a friendship and a business relationship for something near a decade now, and when he told me what happened, I was shocked. In fact, shocked is a junk word for what I was; traumatized is better. Part of me had trouble believing it. Cancer is something old people get; not young athletes who leg press a thousand pounds.

Oh, and do us both a favor, and don't write to me about that last sentence. I know that's not true. I know that cancer impacts people of all ages and all conditions, but I don't care who you are, nobody expects brain cancer in an otherwise healthy 28 year old; and it hit me like a brick.

It was probably harder for David's wife Caren, and all the rest of his family and loved ones, but still.

◆◆◆

"My perspective?" he replied. "My perspective was that it sucked, but not in the way I think anybody would expect."

"In what way?" I asked.

"Okay, so, you know how with cancer diagnoses everybody is thinking 'oh man I'm going to die'?"

"Sure," I replied, "I imagine that is a pretty normal response."

"Right, and it is," he said. "But, I figured I would beat it. I knew there was going to be work. I knew there was going to be suffering. But it didn't really matter, because I would beat it. So, there I am, expecting to live life, while everybody is treating me like I'm dying tomorrow. I really just wanted everybody to toughen up a bit."

"Real problems," I replied, happy to know that he could take a joke.

"Yeah, first world at its finest," he replied. "I mean, I had real problems; I had brain cancer. But I wasn't looking at that. I was looking at living life, fighting, continuing to work, continuing to help the world. And all everybody else was doing was trying to figure out if I was in denial or not."

"Were you?"

"No. At least not that I know of," he replied, laughing at himself.

"Were you working because you were worried about the costs?" I asked.

"No, I was working because I have a job to do."

I was unsure if he was being honest, so I asked him if

the costs were even a thought.

"The costs were a thought, but not a worry," he replied. Look, making money is easy once you know how to do it. I knew this was going to be gigantic, and possibly take time to pay off, but I also knew I would find a way."

♦♦♦

I know. The great majority of you, as readers, if you've never experienced Dave before, have to be sitting there thinking that this guy is either oblivious because he's rich, or foolish. I assure you, it's not quite either of those.

Dave's been rich, and he's been poor. Thankfully, he knows how to make money, and he knows how to do it quickly. That is why I tell you that while his cavalier attitude towards hundreds of thousands of dollars in medical bills may seem foolish, it's not. It comes from his perspective that he will be able to solve the problem; and as far as the cost of the first surgery went, he was right.

♦♦♦

"I remember visiting you and being shocked by the computer setup."

"There was work to be done," he replied.

When I visited him, David was in a private hospital room, and next to his bed sat his computer, and two big screen monitors, all setup so that he could run his business from the hospital. It came as no surprise, but it certainly confirmed what I thought about him; he's crazy, in the greatest way possible.

"Why did you think that you had to work like that?" I asked.

"Why wouldn't I work?" he replied.

"I don't know, maybe because you were about to have your skull cut open and didn't know if you'd be able to speak when you woke up. Or, how about the fact that if the slightest thing went wrong, you could have woke up paralyzed? Or, that it was pretty much a guarantee that there would be some sort of complications coming out of brain surgery, and you may have just wanted to spend that time with family and loved ones? I'll tell you this, if it were me, any of those reasons may have had me not paying much attention to work."

"That's a lie," he said. "I know you. You'd have been taking clients until they cut you open."

He might be right, but I certainly don't know.

"Maybe," I replied, "but what was it really? I might work with clients, but that's only because I'm trying to help people. I know you though. You aren't actually worried about some random real estate deal. You don't actually *need* to make the next deal happen. So, why work hard in that scenario?"

"For the same reason we are writing this book," he replied, smiling at me like the Cheshire cat.

"To help people?" I asked.

"Exactly."

As usual, Dave and I were sitting across from each other, me asking questions, him answering them, and me typing as fast as I could in a vain attempt to keep up with the conversation. As I typed, I noticed that his eyes were fixed on my keyboard.

"Thoughts?" I asked.

"You type fast."

"Kind of have to," I replied.

"Yeah, but you *can* type fast. It takes me about three

minutes to write one line of an email."

What Dave said was true. During our first interview he asked me to pause for a moment so he could make some notes. He opened his computer and began to type, and about five minutes later he was finished. He had written out about fifty words, in five minutes. His right hand was recovering, and he could at least type, but speed was not a part of the equation yet.

"That's true," I replied, "you're slow, but keep in mind, just one month ago you couldn't type at all, yet alone slowly. Crap, a month ago you could barely flick a light-switch."

"No kidding," he replied. "I'm just noting how far back I am."

"Does it bother you?" I asked, knowing the answer.

"Hell yes. And, hell no," he replied.

"Because you could, but can't?" I asked.

Dave gave me a funny look, the type of look you give someone when you are trying to figure out what they are really up to.

"Is this for the book?" he asked.

"Yes," I replied. "Just because I know it, doesn't mean the reader knows it."

"Yeah, well let's make it crystal clear," he replied. "Yes, for a moment, I was bothered because there was a time I could type fast, and now I can't. But that's not the problem anymore. Now, it's just that I want to grow, faster. I want to get better. And yeah, I know that I am getting better, but I want to get better, faster."

◆ ◆ ◆

Let me tell you something. When I tell you that Dave is indomitable, I mean it. In fact, I'm saddened by the fact that there isn't a better word for what he is. What he actually is, is something along the lines of indomitable, unstoppable, immovable, and more. But, the interesting part about Dave, is *why* he is these things. You see, it's not because he's actually strong, or special, or uniquely built in some way that only he can be. It's because he's like one of those stupid wonderful punching bags that we get for children where it's a giant balloon that you can hit, knock over, and it just floats right back up. That's Dave. He gets knocked over, but he just gets right back up. No matter what. He doesn't know how to not. When cancer kicked his butt, he didn't know how to just lay down and die. All he knows how to do, is to get back up and fight again. And because of that, most of the time, he wins.

◆ ◆ ◆

"Forget about the typing," he said. "It's coming back. Tell that to the reader. Tell them that if we meet, they should ask me to type something out in front of them, and I will. I'll get my typing right back to where it was, maybe better."

Playing the part of Captain Downer, I reminded Dave that we don't really know that he will ever get it back in full; the typing speed, that is.

"Sure we do," he replied. "We just don't know how far."
"Exactly. You might get it all back, and be typing a hundred words per minute, but, you might never top 30 words per minute ever again. Are you sure you want people to challenge you to type in front of them?"
"I'm not racing them for speed," he replied. "Who knows how fast I'll get? I certainly don't know. But, I know that I'll have done everything possible to recover my speed, and that's what I would be showing off."
"That you tried?" I asked.

"Exactly. Who care's how fast I get? All I care about is that I gave it my all to get fast. The method is what gets results, so I brag about the method, and that's all. That's where I win in something like this, in the strategy, in the effort, in the will. Not in the end result; that would just be stupid."

Sitting on David's table was a glove designed specifically for people with motor-disfunctions like his. The glove is designed to be worn while playing a game that helps to build fine motor movement, with the goal of assisting in the ability to perform tasks such as typing on a keyboard. His occupational therapy lab had it, so he bought it. Because it seemed to help (and, likely did).

"You could carry around the glove?" I suggested.

"Nah, it's a tool. It's a good example of rule six, but a crap example of will. Owning the fact that I'm whatever I am is a way better method to show people will. And, perhaps rule five," he replied.

"Because you could afford it?" I asked, referring to his comment about it being a good example of rule six.

"Exactly. That thing was three hundred and fifty dollars. If I was poor, I wouldn't have been able to buy it, and there's no way my recovery would be going as well as it is."

"Hence, rule six, get free," I replied.

"Exactly, and that's why I wanted to do the success book. It pisses me off that I can do things like this, and others can't. I don't want anyone to suffer more than they have to, and it sucks that because they never learned how to make money, that they can't get the same quality of care."

"Agreed," I replied. "In fact, I think most everybody agrees. That's probably why there are so many people across America that want socialized medicine."

"Yeah, but let's not go there. That's a powder keg I

don't want to mess with. One day, that might be the case. Whether it will be a good thing, or a total catastrophe, who knows? We shall see. What I do know is that we wouldn't even have to talk about it if people knew how to make money. 'Poor Man Bob' wouldn't need socialized medicine if he wasn't 'Poor Man Bob'. So, let's just show him how to become 'Rich Man Bob'. It's much easier."

David M. Prentice and Joshua M. Gordon

SOMETHING THAT WORKS

"Do you want to talk about your first surgery?" I asked.

"Nah, there's not much to talk about. They did it, the surgeon was great, I looked like somebody beat me with a baseball bat, and then I recovered."

If you want to understand David Prentice, this is a quintessential example. Here we are, talking about brain surgery, and Dave's treating it like it was nothing more than a bad night at the bar.

"We should talk about it just a bit more," I suggested. "People are likely to be interested."

"To hear about me laying in a hospital bed?" he asked.

"I know you're joking," I replied, "but yes, some people are going to want to know that you spent six days in that hospital bed barely able to move. They'll want to know what you actually had to go through, if anything, at least so that they can understand you better. The reader will want to know what it was like. It's part of the human condition."

"Perverse curiosity?" Dave asked.

"No, it's the intrigue of suffering," I replied.

Dave asked me if what I meant by 'the intrigue of suffering', was how people tend to be interested in seeing people suffer.

"Kind of," I replied, "but not exactly. It definitely sounds perverse when you say it like that, but it's not a perverse thing. It's the fact that we all suffer in some way, and because we know that future suffering is inevitable, we like to see how other people respond to it. It's informative. It helps us. It's a way for us to prepare for those moments where we have to face our own trials. It's nothing perverse, it's simply preparation."

"Alright, that makes sense," he replied. "If it helps, I'll tell them all about my suffering. So, here goes. Day one, I couldn't speak. They had me on five different pain killers. It was something like 30 pills a day, plus the intravenous stuff. I was so messed up, that I don't even know when I began to move again."

'Beginning to move again' is Dave's awfully shorthanded way of referencing the moment when he regained at least some function in his extremities. For a short period of time, he was little more than comatose.

♦ ♦ ♦

I'll never forget my first visit to Dave's hospital room. I remember vividly walking into the hospital, wondering what I was going to see. Was I going to see him lying in bed, near death? Was I going to see him laughing and playing cards? I didn't know. What I did know, was that I was nervous, and I don't usually get nervous.

Entry to his room brought a pleasant and surprising sight. Dave was sitting up in his bed, in regular street clothes, like nothing was wrong. It was surprising, and refreshing. Here he is having just found out he has brain cancer, and he's looking like it was just any other Tuesday. It was a great sight to see, him being in good spirits and all, but the real comedy took place a few moments later, when I noticed the contents of a box sitting on the ground next to his bed. In this box, sat computer equipment, clothes, work files, and a foam roller.

If you don't know what a foam roller is, it is nothing more than a foam cylinder that people can use to get rid of muscle knots (those are the things massage therapists work on). Years back I showed Dave how to use one, and encouraged him to use it to restore some flexibility issues he was having.

So, to be clear, David was in the hospital, for a brain tumor, was told that he was going to have a surgery where there is a very real chance he might wake up paralyzed, and he was still working on improving his flexibility.

That was the moment that I realized that Dave is either completely nuts, or a genius.

♦♦♦

"What about the foam roller?" I asked. "Did you get any use out of it?"

He told me that before the surgery he used it regularly. After the surgery, obviously not.

"What about your recovery?" I asked. "You ready to spend some time on that?"

"That's another 'why bother'," he replied.

"Really? You couldn't walk properly, you could barely use your right hand, and then what, six months later you pulled off a 1,000 pound leg press, and you think that's not worth bothering telling people about?"

"1,017 pounds," he replied, emphatically, "and it was three months after the surgery, not six. But yeah, not worth talking about."

"Any reason?" I asked.

"Because it's just part of the journey. Who cares if the journey is 'glorious'? I care about the method more than anything, and that number, and any speed at which I achieved it, was a product of the method, so let's talk about that. Forget about the number, let's focus on the method."

♦ ♦ ♦

Well, Dave might want to skip the story, but I most certainly do not. It's too good, so I'm sharing it.

June 26, 2018, Dave goes in for his first brain surgery. In July, his recovery work began. Come August, with the post-surgery inflammation dying down, and him progressing at an insanely fast rate, Dave decides that he is going to start running again, and promptly sprains his ankle.

Fast forward to September. Dave restarts his leg work, focusing primarily on stability due to the damaged ligaments from the running incident. By September 8th, his leg was stable enough to start working with heavier weights. His first day back lifting heavy ended with a 505 pound leg press, though it was at a much reduced range.

David's exercise history is long, and it is important to note that before his surgery, a full range 505 pound leg press would have been good work for him, but far from what he was capable of. What neither of us expected, was what would happen on October 6, 2018.

Fourteen weeks after brain surgery, and only one month into heavy lifting, Dave pulled off a personal best 1017 pounds on a leg press. For those who don't want to do the math, that's 462.27 kilos Over half a ton. Or, for a really fun way to look at it, more weight than an original brand new half-ton pickup truck could handle.

Dave would demand that I told you that he only got one full rep, and then failed miserably on the second rep, but that's just because he's obsessed with the process over the result. But, I will also note that we were only targeting one rep, not two.

David's insane recovery was the product of a lot of

things, but what it really came down to was the fact that Dave just doesn't know how to quit. If he was asked to do something, he did everything he could to do it. If he failed, he failed trying his best.

The results were the combination of the right knowledge, the right will, and the right mindset, all coming together in perfect harmony. And, while he might not want to talk about it, I just had to.

Dave leg pressing 650% of my bodyweight...
Only 14 weeks after brain surgery
♦ ♦ ♦

"You know I'm going to put it in the book?" I said.

"Of course I know you are going to put it in the book," he replied. "But that's okay, that way it's you bragging, not me."

Did I mention Dave's crafty?

I suggested that we move on and talk about the method, which he of course was all for.

"You were there," he said. "You know what the training was like. If you think it would be good for the book, put it in there."

"We aren't going to tell people about the training

protocols, we're going to focus on the mental," I replied. "We need to talk about the heart. The will. Those are the things that people want to know about, not if you should do exercise A before exercise B, or what speed they should be done at."

"Okay," he replied, "makes sense. Training protocols would be different for everybody anyways."

"Indeed. So, tell me about the method. The mental portion, the heart portion," I said.

"Well, I feel like I'm just repeating myself here, but the method is simple; win."

"No," I replied, "winning is the byproduct. We need to talk about *how* you did it."

"Look, the success I had with my recovery was the product of the same thing that's given me my success with business. I follow some simple rules, and they work every time."

"Okay, what are those rules?" I asked, wondering if I was about to have to write ten chapters just to answer one question.

"They're easy," he replied. "Rule one, figure out what matters. Once you've done that, move to rule two; surround yourself with people that will be positive influences. Rule three, set goals. Four, be courageous. Follow that up with rule five, and start failing, but do it properly. And finally, rule six, get free."

"That was pretty fluid," I said. "I take it you've said that more than once in life."

"I have, but it's not really a mantra, just an approach. After all, what would the acronym for that be, FSSBFG? That's not exactly memorable," he replied.

"No, definitely not too memorable, but it works, so, maybe it doesn't have to be a great acronym or a catchy aphorism. Maybe, it can just be something that works."

"Yep," he said.

I asked if he thought that was all there was to it.

"Yep," he replied.

Standard David Prentice. When something is simple, it's simple. That's it.

"And that's really what you wanted this book to be about, right?"

"Yeah," he replied, "because who cares about my story. Neither Bob the real estate investor nor Susie cancer survivor care about me, they just want to be rich like me and survive like me. It's not my story they care about, it's achieving what I've achieved. Crap, I don't even care about my story."

"I care about your story," I replied.

"Yeah, because we are friends," he said.

"No, that's why I care about *you*. But I'm not talking about you, I'm talking about your story. You have to realize that your story is the type of thing that actually matters; it's the type of story that can save lives."

"How so?" he asked.

"Because despite you being so pragmatic in the face of a death sentence, most people aren't. Most people, when told they might have a month to live, don't start analyzing how to beat the system. They can't. But you did. And that's the reason we are here, still alive, still thriving, still growing, and able to have this conversation. There's somebody out there right now who is going to get some terrible news sometime soon, and your story may be a significant part of them not giving up. So, that matters."

"Okay, my story matters," he replied. "So, should we skip how I did it all and just tell them about my life?"

"No," I replied, "definitely not. If it matters, we're going to include it. And, if we do our job right, we can both tell your story, and tell them how you did it. Hopefully."

"And the economic advice? The real estate guidance? Are we tossing that?" he asked.

"No, because that's part of how you succeeded," I replied.

"Get rich and don't die. The memoirs of David Prentice. Got it," he said.

"I think we will need something else for the title," I replied. "It is better than FSSBFG though."

IF WE WANT TO SUCCEED

"How firmly do you stick to your rules?" I asked.

"As firmly as I'm capable," he replied. "But I'm dumb, so I screw it up all the time."

"Yet you have still found a great deal of success."

"Yeah, because when it's a good approach, you don't have to bat a thousand; and thank God for that, because nobody gets it right each and every time. I mean, think about it, great baseball players don't hit the ball every time they get up to the plate. If you could hit the ball 4 out of 10 at bats, you're amazing. Life's no different."

"Then why call them rules?" I asked.

"Because they are how we *should* do things. Just because I'm a screw up and fail at it, doesn't change that this is what we should do if we want to succeed."

"Let's break the rules down a little bit, can we do that?"

Smirking at me, he replied, "If you're willing to put it in the book."

♦♦♦

Dave's comment about if I would or would not be willing to put it in the book, was an ongoing rib between the two of us. Before we started this project, we sat down to discuss editorial control. For those who don't know, editorial control is a fancy way to talk about who gets the final call on something when there is a disagreement. Think of whether or not we include the story about the time he (fill in the blank). That decision, to include or not include the story, goes to the person who has editorial control. As for us, and our choice of who gets it, foolishly, we never finalized a decision. While we both based it on the fact that we didn't expect to run into any disagreements, it was really because he and I both knew that he would likely defer to me if I thought it should be included. It was this unspoken awareness that led to regular joking about if I would allow something into the book or not.

♦ ♦ ♦

"You mentioned your rules in order. Is there actually an order, or is it just how you said them?"

"No, there's an order," he replied. "I don't know when I realized there was an order, but there definitely is one."

"Then let's follow that order. Step one, figuring out what matters; tell me about that."

"You should do it," he replied, giving me a good chuckle.

"No kidding," I said, "but, why is figuring out what matters rule number one, and not rule number two? Or three for that matter?"

"Because you can't do any of the other steps right if you haven't done step one. If you don't first figure out what matters, everything else gets screwed up."

Dave went on to give me this great analogy about driving a car. The idea is that if you start driving before you've picked a destination, you're just going to end up in some random spot, and odds are good it won't be ideal. "Even the most powerful car in the world, driven without direction, is only going to get you chaos," he said. "It might be fun for part of the time, but it sucks real bad when you then have to drive 3000 miles back to get to where you actually want to be in life."

"I get that," I replied, "and I like the analogy, but, wouldn't surrounding yourself with good people help with that? They could help you in choosing a destination. Or, goal in this case. Maybe that should be first?"

"Nope," he replied.

"Alright, I'll bite. Why? Why is it better to figure out what matters, before surrounding yourself with positive influences?"

"Because," he replied, "when it comes to who you should surround yourself with, there isn't enough time in the day to not be picky. You have to pick the specific people you *need* to surround yourself with. It's just part of the demands of time."

I asked Dave what he meant by 'needing' to surround yourself with specific people.

"It's like this," he began, "you only have so much time to surround yourself with the people who will influence you, so, you have to specialize. Let's say you want to be the world's best baker. You go, and surround yourself with some of the most amazing people in the world, but none of them are amazing at baking. In fact, these people, the ones you've surrounded yourself with, while yeah, they're awesome, they're area of specialization is software programming. What does that do for you? You aren't trying to be a programmer. You are trying to be a baker. You need to surround yourself with amazing bakers. That's why rule one is rule one, because all of that is dependent on you knowing what you want to be."

"Okay, makes sense," I replied. "First things first, what

matters."

We sat there for a moment, just silent. Dave was waiting for me to ask the next question, but there was a problem. I wasn't sure if we were ready to move on from rule one. Not just yet at least. After a moment, I knew what was being left out.

"You know what, Dave, I'm not sure we're ready to move on from that."

"Okay," he replied.

"We've skipped a pretty important detail. What about the question of *when* you should apply the rules?"

"Easy," he replied. "Anytime you want something to change, you apply the rules. Looking to change your career? Apply the rules. Trying to save a relationship? Apply the rules. Trying to grow a business on your own? Apply the rules. Even with something little like choosing where you are going to go for dinner. If you want the best results, apply the rules."

"So, if you want change, apply the rules," I replied. "And, I guess somewhat obviously, the answer of what matters, is tied to whatever it is that you are trying to change."

"Yep," he replied.

"But, there's a problem," I said.

To which he replied that there wasn't.

"No, there is. Let's say you are trying to change both your family life, and your work life. You want more family time, and you also want a promotion, which at your job, means more time at work. They contradict each other. What then?"

"You make goal two fit into goal one," he replied.

"Combine them?" I said, in a way that was part statement, part question.

"Yeah," he said, "but this is horrible in text, just send people to the website."

NOTE TO THE READER: In the original plan, the website, along with graphics to help explain this idea, would have been up and running when you read this. That will not be the case now. Thankfully, you should get a good idea of what he's talking about from what follows.

"I'll do that, but let's give them an overview," I replied.

"Alright, it's a bit like the outline of a book. The book has a main goal, and then each chapter has its own goal. In life, if the main answer to 'what matters' is family, then the subsections are probably career, hobbies, etc. Those subsections are the chapters of the book that we call your life. And, just like an outline of a book, they all have to work together."

"They have to fit," I replied.

"Exactly. Chapter one has to fit into the confines of the book's mission. If your life mission is family, then career has to be organized within the confines of 'family'. It's that simple. Take this book for example. In this book, the main mission is to help people. The answer to rule number one, is help people. But, we have an additional goal, we want to make the book enjoyable to read. Two goals, and they have to fit together. If we told really entertaining stories, then in a way, we could help people, but not in the way we are talking about. Our goal, of helping people learn how to be conquerors, to be survivors, to thrive, demands more than the entertainment of fiction. So, while fictional stories might make for great entertainment, in this case, the entertainment must fall behind the main mission of ensuring that we are helping people. Get it?"

"I do," I replied.

"Good," he said.

I suggested that we were ready to move on to rule two, to which Dave disagreed.

"We aren't ready for rule two. Not yet. We need to talk about value. Specifically, how to figure out if something is or isn't valuable."

I told him that I thought most people already understand that. At least the type of people that would be reading this book, that is.

"They'll know all about economic value," he replied, "but they may not realize that there is a monstrous difference between achievement and fulfillment, and that if they never learn the difference, their life is going to suck. They'll have all the money in the world, and be miserable. How stupid would that be?"

"Pretty stupid," I replied.

Dave was getting wound up. We were getting into one of his favorite topics, and you could see that he was excited. He paused to promise me that he would keep it short. It's Dave, I believed him.

"I'm not too worried about you keeping things succinct. And you don't have to worry about the length, if it's worth it, we'll put it in," I replied.

"I'll still keep it short," he said. "It's like this. Achievement, is the product of a science that can be learned for almost everything that exists. Health, money, you name it, there's a science to achieving it. That means that no matter the goal, odds are good that somebody has figured out how to do it, and all you have to do is mirror what they did. If you do that, in most cases, you will have what they have. That means that you don't have to reinvent the wheel, just duplicate it. Simple. If you want to succeed, it's easy. The problem though, is that while success is nice, on its own, it isn't actually valuable. The only type of success that is valuable, is the type that provides fulfillment, and that requires planning. And not just planning, but thinking, and understanding. Rule one lets you figure out how to find fulfillment. If it matters to you, and you apply the science needed to achieve it, then you can have what is really valuable; fulfillment."

"That is simple," I replied.

"Right. You figure out what matters, and then you figure out how to do it."

"What if you can't figure it out?" I asked.

"Hire a coach, that's what I do. When I didn't know how to walk, I hired a coach. When I didn't know how to succeed, I hired a coach. When you don't know how to do something, all you have to do is find someone who does, and convince them to help you. Then, learn how to do it, then do it, and be fulfilled. Nothing more complex than that," he said.

"Sounds good to me," I replied. "Are we ready for rule two then?"

"Don't we need to include goal drift?" he asked.

"Oh. I think we kind of have to," I replied.

"Yeah, but yuck," he said. "If it means anything, I'd rather not have to cover it."

"We can be brief," I said, "but I'm betting most people have never thought about it."

"I'm sure they haven't, " he replied. "Up until I was taught it, I certainly never noticed it."

"Alright, well, as you do, keep it simple, and let's get through it."

"Sounds good," he said, "especially since it is simple. The gist of it is that goal drift is when you start out with a mission, begin working towards it, start succeeding, and then forget why you were doing whatever it is that you were doing. Basically, it's when the mission gets lost."

"Got it," I replied, reflecting on how often that occurs when I'm writing.

"Good, then let's move on."

"Okay, but first, what is it about goal drift that causes you to hate it so much?"

"Easy," he replied, "it's cost me millions of dollars."

"Ouch. I guess if it had cost me millions of dollars I wouldn't want to talk about it either."

"Yeah, so let's move on."

"Okay, let's say that Bob sits down, reads this book, and says 'that's good, Dave's right, I need to have a direction.' Once he's said that, what's his next step?"

SIT DOWN...AND THINK

To the question of what someone should do once they've agreed that they need to have a direction, Dave gave me a particularly short answer. I asked for him to expand on it, and he gave me this.

"It's not that complex," he said. "Once somebody has realized that they need to figure out what matters, if they want to do it, all that they need to do is to sit down, shut up, and think."

Yep, that's Dave when he gets complex. And I'll tell you this, while it's really nice to have someone teach you something with such simplicity, it certainly makes it difficult to write a book about it.

"Nothing else?" I asked.

"Nope," he replied. "That's what they need to do. If you've realized that you need a direction, the next thing to do, is to think."

"About what?" I asked.

"About what matters," he replied. "They need to write it out, on paper, and then really, truly, think about it. Forget about the canned answers that pageant contestants give. Think about what matters to you, write it out, and then think about it even more."

"Is it really that simple?" I asked.

"No, but yes," he said. "Look, most people suck at self-evaluation. I know that for the longest time, I most certainly was horrible at it, and, if I'm being honest, I debate if I'm even good at it now. So, if we all suck at self-evaluation, we likely also suck at figuring out what matters. But, that's why you write it out. That's why you think about it not once, not twice, but many times. And that's why you have to come back to it from time to time, because number one, you might screw it up, and number two, things change."

Dave's teaching style never fails to give me a laugh. While most people worry about coordinating their words to 'sell' ideas, Dave just chucks it out there. I'm convinced that his method only works because it is backed up by more life experience at his young age than many will have in their entire lifetime. If anybody else were to teach the way he does, I'm not so sure it would work. That's assuming they don't have some massive life experience behind them, that is.

"Alright, so, sit down, brainstorm, evaluate, re-evaluate. Got it. What's next?" I asked.

"Remember, we are talking about making a grand big picture of life here. I'm not saying that if somebody wants to apply the rules to what pizza place their going to order from that they need to put this much thought into anything, I'm just talking about in the beginning, when someone is deciding on a lifepath. So, for something as serious as a lifepath, once they've done the thinking, and finalized it, the next thing they need to do is simply wait one week."

"One week?" I replied.

"Yeah. Wait a week," he said. "Every morning, take at least ten minutes, and think about what life looks like if your life was dedicated to that one particular purpose. At the end of a week, if your answer hasn't changed, you've got the big picture rule one handled."

Dave's Challenge #1

It's time to stop watching life fly by, and start choosing a direction. Challenge #1 is to take the time to find your answer to rule #1. What matters to you? What drives you? What is it, that if you knew you were waking up today to focus on, you'd wake up excited and ready to go? What would make every day feel like the best day ever? That will be your answer to rule #1, that will be your mission, and we challenge you to figure it out.

Take time today, sit down, shut up, and think. Think about what really matters, and then write it down. Once you've done that, spend the next week taking 10 minutes each day, preferably in the morning, and think about your mission, and what life would look like if you dedicated your intentions towards it. Perhaps it's your family. What would life look like if your work schedule was dictated by your family goals, instead of *just* your financial goals? Perhaps it's your health. Think about how life would go if you not only knew you desired something, but planned and drove for that thing, achieving it as the byproduct of your efforts. No matter what your answer is, just know this:

It's time to stop 'not dying', and start thriving.

On day three, in that same ten minute window, start to think about what needs to happen so that your life can point you to your answer to rule #1. Do you need to adjust your work schedule? Your diet? Your television time? Whatever it is, figure it out, and if you can't, find someone who can help coach you along on it.

On the seventh day, if your answer hasn't changed, commit yourself to it. Tell the world about it. Go on social media and tell everybody that you are going to live your life committed to your mission. After that, write it down on the lines below.

My Rule #1:

_____

_____

_____

If you are reading this on an eBook, don't skip writing it down just because you can't (or at least shouldn't) write on your screen. Get a notepad or a piece of paper, and write it down. The same goes for all the other challenges as well. Writing it down matters, do not skip this step, you will be missing out, drastically. The more places you commit yourself to your mission, the better, so find every spot you can tell anyone about it, and do so.

If you are going to use social media to do it, which we highly recommend, use the hashtag #watchdavewin so that everybody can find out, offer encouragement, and join you on your journey to a better life.

◆ ◆ ◆

"Got it," I replied. "Then, is that it? Anything left for rule one?"

"Nope. As long as they've seen the content about how one piece fits with another, there's nothing left on rule one."

"Perfect," I replied, "because that means we can move on to your childhood."

"Or," said Dave, "we could just move on to rule two."

"Nah, we need to spend some time on your past. We can't just skip it like it's irrelevant."

"It's not that interesting," he replied.

"Is anybody's?"

"Hmm," he said, "I don't know."

"Well, I don't either, but I know that people need to know about it."

"Why?" he asked.

♦ ♦ ♦

Dave does this thing when he thinks he is about to learn something. He kind of tips his head back at the top, lifting his chin up and twisting it just to the side. His lips purse together, and then the real give away comes. His eyes tell you what he's expecting. And the best part about it, is that there's an excitement hiding behind them, and it's obvious.

In a world filled with people who are busy pretending they know everything; Dave relishes the opportunity to be a student. In those moments, it's clear that he knows he's about to learn something that is going to improve his life, and he loves it. The man is undoubtably more interested in gathering the facts that make life better, than nearly anything else, and it's pretty cool to see.

♦ ♦ ♦

"The 'why' is easy," I replied. "People need to hear about your childhood because they need to know not just who you are, but where you came from. Without it, they won't know that your advice can actually help them. They'll be stuck with the myriad of assumptions that we all bring to the table. Maybe you were born into wealth? Maybe you're some genius wonderkid who skipped ten grades and graduated from Harvard at age 13? Until we tell them, they have no idea how much you have survived. I know that if I only knew your current situation, and didn't know your past, it would drastically affect my ability to learn from your life. That's why we have to talk about your childhood."

"I get that," he replied, "but, isn't it who I am now that actually matters? I mean, yeah, my childhood taught me things, but it won't teach the reader anything but not to be an idiot. Most people already know that."

"Sure they do, but that's not the only thing your story provides. When the reader finds out that you're a high-school dropout, they can know that they can succeed too, irrelevant to their current education level. When they find out that you come from a divorced family, and that you were living in a trailer park, and all the other wild details that have gone into your crazy life, it's those things that let them know that they can do it too. It will show them that no matter what stage of life they are in, if they are willing to implement your methods, they can have a better life."

"Because it's not actually about me," he said.

"Exactly. Even to us, it's not actually about you."

"Because of rule one," he replied.

Confused how we got back to rule one, I asked Dave what he was talking about.

"I'm talking about figuring out what matters, rule one," he said.

"I remember what rule one is; we were talking about it two minutes ago. I just don't know why you brought it up."

"Because," he said, "when I didn't know why we were going to talk about my childhood, I was failing to remember rule one. It was just a good example."

I stared at him trying to understand. I wish I got it quicker, but, I didn't.

"When we planned out this book, we established our answer to rule one," he said. "We decided that what matters, particularly for this book, was helping people. So, we aren't talking about my childhood because it is interesting, we are talking about it because it helps people."

"Oh, yes. Exactly," I replied, pleased that he understood, and surprised how easily rule one had come into play without me even realizing it.

"Let's just make sure we keep it short," he said. "I mean, I hear what you're saying, but if we want to help people, we can probably just stick to the major details of my childhood. Let's not let it turn into filler and put it in there just to pull on people's heart strings. I don't like filler."

"I don't like filler either," I replied, "but this isn't filler. You have to remember, more often than not, it's people's scars that are what hold them back. There is some person out there who comes from a divorced family just like yours, and they haven't reconciled that with their life. That person truly thinks that they cannot make it in life because of their parents' divorce. When that person finds out that your parents were divorced when you were just a toddler, and they see that you have succeeded, it gives that person evidence that they could do it too."

"Like Cheryl Broyles," Dave replied.

"Who?"

"Cheryl Broyles."

"No, I heard you, I just don't know who that is."

"Cheryl Broyles, along with Jane McClellan, Ben Williams, and countless other survivors, are all part of the reason I'm alive."

"I have a feeling there's a story behind that comment," I said.

"Of course there is."

I saw David's eyes light up, which was fun, and I got ready to type at what I assumed was going to be a very rapid pace. What this had to do with people's emotional scars, I had no clue, but I was looking forward to finding out.

Dave began, "When I got the second diagnosis, and they told me that I might die in less than a month, lots happened, but one of the things, was that I found out about Cheryl, and the fact that she was still alive 19 years after she was diagnosed with a glioblastoma. Then I heard about Jane McClellan. Jane's this awesome woman who wrote a book on different approaches to cancer, and it inspired me to take control of my medical care, which is what got me to the doctors I'm currently working with. These are the doctors who are doing such an amazing job at keeping me alive, and if it weren't for Jane, I don't know that I would have ever found Dr. Friedman."

I asked David what it was about Cheryl's survival that had impacted him.

"The way I see it, even if pretty much everybody dies from this, if she could survive, I could survive."

"Good thing she told her story," I replied.

"Yeah," he said, "and you know what, if she never told her story, if she never shared it, I might not have known it was possible. I might have spent the next month wallowing away until I died."

"You mentioned another name, Ben Williams. Who's that?" I asked.

"Oh man, Ben is the biggest winner of them all. The man was diagnosed with a glioblastoma something like 25 years ago. Less than 9% of people make it past two years, and there he is, kicking butt and taking names 25 years later. That man is winning, and I love it."

"So, their story, their experiences, are part of your survival. I get it. With that in mind, do you now see why your story matters?" I asked.

"I do," he replied, "but I make no promises about it being interesting."

♦ ♦ ♦

I have to step out of the story for a moment. I need to say this. What you are reading, is a factual account. Cheryl Broyles is not a made up individual. Nor is Ben Williams, nor is Jane McClellan. They aren't characters being added to the book in order to provide for drama. They are real people, and their existence, their fight, and their will to share what was going on in their survival, is partially responsible for my friend being alive. Because of that, I'd like to say to Cheryl, Jane, Ben, and all of the others who have been willing to share their stories, from the bottom of my heart, I thank you.

Before we get back to the book, there is one more thing I need to say. Most of us think that our lives aren't that interesting, and because of that, we don't have anything to say. But, that's crap. It's not true. Everybody has value. Everybody has something to add.

Don't hesitate to speak up, you might just be somebody else's Cheryl.

"Alright, so can we talk about your childhood now?"

David M. Prentice and Joshua M. Gordon

AN 8 YEAR OLD JERK

"Where should we start?" he asked.

I told Dave that we needed to talk about the events that formed him; the challenges, the struggles, the chaos, all of that. He replied by asking me if I wanted to talk about his 'pain points'.

"I want everything," I replied. "I want pain points, I want history, I want craziness. If it's about your past, I want to hear about it."

"There isn't space," he replied.

"I know. We won't be including everything, but, when we look at our own lives, we tend to be poor judges of the parts that matter to other people. We focus on the things that were big impacts on ourselves, and miss the things that could be big impacts on others. So, just tell me about your childhood, and I'll leave out the stuff that is less important. In the book, we'll focus on the stuff that matters, but for now, let's just get it all out there."

"Good luck," he replied. "There's a bunch."

"Yes, I know," I said.

♦♦♦

A quick note for readers: Pain points is just a marketing term. It's a way of talking about the problems that a product or service solves. 'Hard to clean dishes' is a pain point for advertising dish soap. 'Sore muscles' is a pain point for a massage advertisement. Whatever the problem is, that is the pain point. The idea of pain point advertising is to highlight that your product or service will relieve the pain. It's effective, but often manipulative.

◆◆◆

"Okay," he began, "here goes. Age three, my parents get divorced. Age 16, I drop out of high school, and spend the next few years being a fat, lazy, stoner. What else do you want to know?"

"There's more," I said. "What happened between age 3 and age 16?"

"I did the same thing every other stupid kid does. I partied, I hung out with friends, tried to meet girls. There's really not much to it."

"Alright, I'll be specific, because there's still more. You said your parents got divorced when you were three, right?"

"Yeah," he said.

"Do you think it affected you?"

With zero hesitation he replied that it had. "Absolutely," he said. I asked if he could tell me how.

"You know what the biggest problem was? They didn't think the same way. It's a big part of why they got divorced. Worse than that though, when they were raising me, they were both doing things differently."

"Like what?" I asked.

"Not everything, but practically everything. One of my parents would teach me something, and the other would go and teach me the opposite. One would use one method, and the other would use a completely different one. It's kind of ironic, but now, they get along great; but not 27 years ago. Back then, they didn't get along at all, and as a kid, it was all just very confusing."

"I imagine," I replied. "How did you figure out what to do?"

"When they disagreed?" he asked.

"Yeah. If one told you to do something, and the other was saying not to, how did you handle that?"

"Like an idiot, just like every other kid," he replied.

"You know Dave, I can speculate on what you mean by that, but, my parents weren't divorced, and I'd rather not assume. What exactly do you mean by 'like an idiot'?"

"It's simple," he replied, "when you are a kid, you don't know anything about long term thinking, so the parent that gives you what you want, is the one you go with."

"Which leaves you spoiled," I said.

"Yeah, except my parents didn't have the means to spoil me with stuff."

"But, you said that you went with the parent that gave you what you wanted. If they didn't have the means to give you material things, what were you talking about? Are you talking about non-material stuff?"

"Yep," he replied. "I wanted stuff, sure, but we were poor, and I was used to it. You know how every Christmas there is some 'must-have' toy that all the children are going crazy over? Yeah, we never thought we were going to be getting that. Which was fine, because it wasn't what I wanted."

"What did you want?" I asked.

"The most valuable thing in history," he replied. "Freedom."

"That's rule 6," I said.
"You got it," he said. "Get free."

I asked Dave how his quest for freedom worked out, and laughed a bit as his eyes rolled at the question.

"Great," he replied, "and, crappy. You see, if I were ever

to have been dumb enough to fight my dad, he would have whooped me, and I knew it. If I wanted to do something, and he didn't want me to, he'd flat out tell me he'd kick my butt, which promptly stopped me from doing it."

"Because of fear?" I asked.

"No, because I'm not that much of a dummy," he replied.

As we sat there, I noticed a woman standing on the sidewalk in front of the house. She was out there, just standing there, staring. The table we were sitting at is in the front room, giving me a perfect vantage point to watch this woman waver back and forth, clearly evaluating if she wanted to come up to the door or not. As she stood there, debating, a little girl, who couldn't have been more than four or five years old stood next to her. Eventually, the woman found the courage and approached. The little girl, who we would soon find out was her daughter, waited for her at the sidewalk.

"There's a woman walking up to the door," I said, remembering that fixing the doorbell was a yet unfinished part of the remodeling project.

Dave had a brief conversation with her. She had noticed that one of the trees above his neighbor's house looked like it was going to fall, and if it did, Dave's home would likely be in its path. Kindly, she wanted to make sure Dave knew. She also left a note for the neighbor.

"That was sweet," I commented.

"Yeah," he replied, "especially because she looked like she was scared silly just ringing the doorbell."

For the record, he's right, she did.

"Pretty cool though," I replied. "I mean, think about it.

That woman was scared, but she didn't let it stop her. Her desire to do something good, was greater than her fear of whatever bad could come from her actions."

"Yep, that woman gets rule four," Dave replied.

"No doubt," I said. "But, let's not go jumping to courage just yet. Let's get back to your quest for freedom."

"You sure?" he replied. "It seems like a pretty good transition point."

"It would be," I said, "if it happened seventy pages from now. But that's not where we are, so let's just get back to your parents and all of that."

"Alright," he replied. "We were talking about my dad not taking my crap, right?"

"We were."

"Okay, so, if I brought some stupid idea to my dad, he would just shut it down. It was easy for him. My mom on the other hand, she couldn't stop me. Maybe she could have kicked my tail, but she never tried, and, as a result, I thought I could do whatever I wanted. You know, I think she meant well, but, I was just too much for her. She couldn't handle me, it's kind of a shame."

"Is that why you lived with her, and not your dad?" I asked.

"Mostly. It's definitely why I wanted to live with her."

"And how did that all work out? Was that a good setup?"

"It depends on how you look at it. I had a bunch of freedom, but I was a kid, and if there's one thing I know from experience, it's that it's not good to give kids too much freedom."

♦♦♦

As a dad, I couldn't agree more, but I must also say that I was shocked that he had realized this. Most of my friends without children tend to miss this fact. Actually, most of my friends with children tend to miss it too.

◆ ◆ ◆

He continued, "I remember one time in particular, and, this actually happened a few times, but there is one time that sticks out pretty strong in my head, where my mom had made dinner, and I didn't want it. I told her I wasn't going to eat it, and she told me what every mother says when their kid says something like that."

I asked if she told him to shut his mouth and eat up.

"Of course," he replied. "But, there was one big problem, I didn't have to. I had a bike, and I had money. So, I told her I was going to go get a pizza, and I did."

"How old were you?" I asked.

"That's the best part; eight. I was eight years old and I was already acting like a jerk."

"How did you have money at eight?"

"I cut lawns," he replied, like it's a normal thing for eight year-olds to have jobs.

"At eight?"

"Yeah. My mom had a push mower, and if I bought gas she would let me take it and mow the lawns for the neighbors."

"Really? At eight years old?"

"Yeah."

"So, I'm guessing you did a lawn or two each week type of thing?"

"No," he replied, "I would usually do like 30 in a week."

"30 lawns per week, with a push mower? What are you talking about?"

"No joke," he replied. "You do know that I'm talking about when we were living in a trailer park, right?"

I hadn't thought about that part. Thirty trailer lawns seemed a lot more reasonable than what I was thinking we were talking about.

"Oh," I replied. "Got it. That makes a lot more sense than what I was thinking."

"Yeah," he said, "and, I was a little kid, so people loved that I was doing something and not just playing video games, so they payed me pretty well for it. I'd get like 10 bucks for a trailer lot. After expenses I was making like 25 bucks an hour, it was great."

Our interview session was pushing into lunch time, and we paused for a moment to grab some food. In an effort to be able to both eat, and interview, I was having a very unexciting protein bar. David, well-motivated by the dangers of cancer, had fashioned for himself (with the help of his wife Caren) a nice plate of chicken and Brussel sprouts.

I told him his food looked good, and asked him if he liked it.

"It's great," he replied. "Tastes like survival."

While I'm not completely sure what survival tastes like, it sounds pretty good.

My very exciting protein bar wrapper.
In the background you can see Dave's wife Caren,
eating a salad the size of a small town. I would have
shown you a picture of Dave's food, but it was gone
before I could think to do so!

"So, you made money, and would buy pizza, and your mom couldn't stop you. Is that about right?"

"Pretty much," he replied.

"Earlier, you said something that surprised me. You mentioned that it was dangerous to give kids too much freedom; which I agree with. But, most of how I learned that came from being a father myself. Considering that you have no children, I take it that you likely learned that lesson the hard way."

"I did," he replied. "I kind of wish I didn't, but I did.

See, the problem was that while I had money, and freedom, I was still an idiot. I didn't know how to use my money wisely. Or my freedom, for that matter. As a result, I did stupid stuff. Lots of stupid stuff. Really, I'm kind of amazed I didn't die or go to jail."

"Now, if my memory serves me right, you didn't stay with your mom. You moved to your dad's at one point, right?"

"Yeah, when I was 12," he said.

"Why'd you change homes?"

"Because I was mad."

"About?" I asked.

"You know what, it was hard. The lifestyle of a broken family, it sucks. You're going back and forth, from this house to that house, from these rules to those rules, and I don't know what to say, it was just really tough. You kind of feel like you have no home base, and no coach. Or, I guess like you have two coaches and they disagree, so you are just out there on the field with no idea which play you are supposed to be making."

"That sounds horrible," I replied, "but, were you mad at the chaos, or at your Mom?"

"It was the chaos. I didn't move to my dad's just because I was mad; there were a lot of things. The anger was just part of it."

"Then, why did you move?" I asked.

David M. Prentice and Joshua M. Gordon

CHAOS

"I moved because my life was chaos," said Dave. "I needed to fix it. My mom had gotten remarried, and they were building a house out in the middle of nowhere. While they were building it, we were living in a camper. Seven of us. Two adults, five children, in a camper. We were sleeping 3 people in one bed, 2 in another, and while it wasn't sheer poverty, it just sucked. Then we had three catastrophic events take place, all within a time period of just one month. It was too much. You know, really, going to my dad's house was an attempt at hitting the reset button."

"Wow. Seven people in three beds, in a camper. That's some tight living," I replied.

"Definitely," he said.

"And those three events, can we talk about them?"

"A bit," he replied, "but only so much, because they affect a lot of people other than me."

I told him I understood, and that we didn't have to include it in the book. He laughed and told me we had to.

"It's the most interesting part of my childhood," he said.

♦♦♦

If you remember from earlier, I mentioned how most

people are poor judges of what will be valuable to others, compared to what is valuable to themselves. As far as this story goes, and it's importance, Dave was right. This was undoubtably the most interesting part of his childhood, and we definitely had to include it. Tragically.

◆◆◆

"First," he began, "we had 9/11. Everybody was freaking out because we just had the largest terrorist attack to ever occur on U.S. soil, and in the midst of that chaos, out of nowhere, my brother Daniel's mom's heart just stops. It's her and my little brothers, with no one else home, and she just drops to the ground, done. She's clinically dead for some massive amount of time while my little brother is freaking out, and, thankfully, my dad just randomly comes home and finds her laying there. I say thankfully because he was able to give her CPR and call 911. When the ambulance arrived, she was gone. It was all a big giant mess. Then the crazy part happens and they were able to revive her. We spend the next two months at the hospital, and day after day, nothing was changing. Unfortunately, she was vegetative, and the doctors were saying there was nothing left that they could do."

David paused himself, I think as a favor to me. He probably saw my face and the shock I was in and thought I needed a moment to collect my thoughts.

"That's insane," I said.
"I'm not done. I haven't even gotten to the really crazy part yet," he replied.

"Okay," I said, shaking my head. "Well, do tell."
"Yeah, so, the doctors say there's nothing left to do, and the decision is made to pull the plug."

Dave paused again. At this point, I think he was just trying to build the drama, which was ridiculous when you think how dramatic the whole event already is; it certainly didn't need anything else.

After his unnecessary dramatic pause, he continued, "And, we did it. We pulled the plug. And then, she started to breathe. On her own."

"What?" I replied, trying to keep my eyes from popping out of my head.

"Yeah, she just started to breathe. Which was good, in a way."

"Why 'in a way?' " I asked.

"Well, she's alive, which is great. But, unfortunately, her brain was severely damaged and now, while she has some function, it's all at an extremely low level. Which is hard. But, to be clear, hard isn't bad, I'm just saying."

"Sure, no, I mean, I get it," I replied.

"And, it was hard for me, but I'm not the focus here. It obviously affected the whole family, but looking back, as an adult, I can't imagine the stress my dad was under. They had five kids, one of which was only seven months old when this happened, and here they are getting slammed with all of the emotional trauma that this is, and that's before you even start thinking about the massive medical bills that they were being hit with."

I didn't reply. Really, because, what on Earth would I have said?

"Anyways," he continued, "that was only two of the things."

"Of three," I replied. "Do I even want to know what the other one was?"

He looked me square in the eyes and with no soft introduction, proceeded to tell me about his grandma dying.

"No joke, she got run over by one of those semi-trucks that carry tens of thousands of pounds of gravel. She was in her car, got smacked by this thing and it ran her over."

"Are you serious?" I asked, now shocked for what was something like the eight-millionth time.

"Yep, a gravel truck," he said. "Sounds like a bad joke, but yeah."

"It does sound like a bad joke," I replied.

"I still remember when I found out. It was in the middle of a band concert. Here I am, my entire life is just one mess after another, and I'm just sitting there playing my instrument when they call me out of the concert. Right in the middle of it. I was sitting there thinking 'oh man, what now? What craziness is this going to be?' And then they tell me about my grandma."

"Those are three crazy, crazy events," I replied.

"Yeah, no matter what definition you like, sixth grade was chaos."

"Alright, so, life is chaos, you move in with your dad in an attempt to get things under control, and then what? What's next?"

"For a while I just floundered around, screwing up. I was busy chasing girls and ignoring school, which eventually led to me dropping out of high school."

"Bit of a jump there," I replied. "Anything in the middle?"

"No," he said. "Not really at least. Basically, all that chaos happened during a time that I was already being an idiot at school. Eventually it just all added up."

I told Dave that his story is a little weird here. He's a smart guy and has this incredible passion for knowledge, yet, he dropped out of school. I told him it didn't really make sense.

"Yeah, I know," he replied, "it's weird. And I know I'll sound like a jerk, but you're right, I am a smart guy. I do stupid stuff all the time, but I am pretty smart when I bother to think. In fact, that's probably the worst part of it all, up until eighth grade, I was a really good student."

"What happened in eight grade?"

"Girls," he replied. "It turns out, they can be really distracting. Like, dangerously distracting. And, between this crap-storm that was my life, and the distractions that I was surrounding myself with, I was just done."

I asked him if there was something that he remembered as maybe being the final straw that led to him dropping out. I wanted to know what broke him, partially because I was shocked he could be broken.

♦♦♦

If you've seen any of the videos we made, you would know that when answering most of our questions, Dave was very quick to respond. Even when faced with questions that were likely painful to answer, Dave was quick. But on this one, he paused. I don't know if he was taking a moment to think about it, or if he was just trying to choose his words carefully, but, for whatever reason, he was slow to respond.

NOTE TO THE READER: Part of the original marketing plan was to release a bunch of videos from the interview process. Due to the circumstances we have found ourselves in, those videos will not have been released by the time this book is published.

"There might have been a last straw," he replied, "but

whether there is or isn't one, it doesn't matter. By the time I got to the point of saying 'I'm done', I was a pretty bad student."

"And?" I asked.

"It didn't really make sense to me."

"What didn't make sense; school, or going?"

"Either," he replied.

I asked Dave why his response was so delayed, and he just sat there for a moment, silent, staring at me with his head tilted off to the side; a position I can only assume was his way of asking me where my question was taking us.

Like the good salesman he is, Dave remained silent until I continued to talk.

"What was running through your head? What were you thinking about?" I asked.

Dave looked around the room as though the answer was floating somewhere in space, just waiting to be grabbed. It was clear that he was thinking, but, about what I didn't know.

"Are you ashamed of it?" I asked.

"I was," he replied, refocusing his attention on me and my keyboard.

"Was?" I asked.

"Yeah," he said. "But, not because I gave a crap. The problem was my girlfriend and my teachers. They all were pretty upset with me, and did a pretty good job of letting their feelings known."

"Such as?" I asked.

"Such as that I was an idiot, and a bum. Which was true. When I was willing to apply myself, school was something I was really good at. But, I wasn't willing to apply myself, so it didn't really matter."

"And now? Are you still ashamed of it?"

"No," he replied, smiling. "Now it's just funny. It worked out. Maybe things would have been better, maybe not, but either way, I'm good. I've succeeded, I've learned. And, while I wouldn't necessarily suggest replicating it, there is no shame left over from it either. It created some good, and some bad, but I'm not ashamed of it."

I asked if there were any particular 'bad things' that stick out to him.

"Sure there is. Like the fact that there's almost no way I could get a normal job," he replied.

"Would you want one?"

"Of course not. That would suck. I'm not made to be an employee. I'm not sure anyone really is."

"It seems like a lot of people prefer being an employee," I said. "I think the idea of avoiding risk is appealing to most people. I imagine that most people look at starting a business, and like the idea of someone else taking on the risk, even if it means they themselves make less money. Maybe those people are made to be employees?"

"Sure," he replied, "maybe. But, I like working for myself, and I don't know anybody who is willing to work hard that doesn't feel the same way. The pros of being your own boss far outweigh the cons. Besides, while it's not a necessity for rule six, it certainly speeds it up."

"Back to getting free," I replied.

"Yeah. But we should mention that being your own boss doesn't mean you are free, it just helps you get there exponentially faster than working for somebody else," he replied.

I mentioned that we were drifting off topic, and that we needed to get back to high school, or the lack there of.

"Before we go and start talking about rule six, tell me

about your parents. How did they respond to you dropping out of high school?"

"You know what, just before I dropped out, I got jumped by a group of seven guys. Guys that were known to cause trouble. Thankfully, I wasn't alone. My friend Carl was with me, and he could handle himself, so it was more like seven on two, but you know."

"This was before you learned how to box though, right?"

"Yeah, but I still had some idea of how to fight. At least, a better idea than these seven guys did."

"Are you saying you won the fight?"

Dave laughed.

"Kind of. I walked away uninjured, and the only damage Carl suffered was a broken hand from smashing it into the face of one of our opponents. So, we kind of won, and at a minimum, we didn't completely get our, umm, rear ends, kicked, so that was good."

"Yeah, I'd say so," I replied.

"Anyways, I was telling you about it because you wanted to know about my parents' response to me dropping out. After we got jumped, my parents understood why I didn't want to be there. My high school wasn't a good place, and they knew it, so that helped make the transition pretty easy."

There's something here that I really hope you see. This is part of what has made Dave successful, and it's rare.

Dave was physically attacked by a group of seven guys, and he sees it as having benefited him. He knows he was a victim, but he doesn't focus on that. He chooses to put his attention towards the benefits that came from the situation.

This is powerful, if you can do this in life, everything,

and I mean *everything*, can be good. That's crazy, but it's awesome. I asked him about his approach, about how he treats having been the victim of an attack like that, and here is what he had to say,

> *"I might have been the victim, but that doesn't mean I can't be the victor, too."*

◆ ◆ ◆

"Did you ever go back to school?" I asked.

"Kind of, but not really."

"What does that mean, 'kind of, but not really'?"

"I took some classes at a community college," he said, "but it wasn't like I was working towards a degree or anything. They were just classes I took because they were about things I wanted to know, and at the time, I thought that was probably the best way to learn."

I asked if he ever thinks about going back. He laughed.

"There's no point now," he replied. "Information is out there, and thankfully with the development of the internet, it doesn't require traditional schooling like it used to. Nowadays if you want to learn something, there is undoubtably some person who's out there doing it, exactly how you want to be doing it, who's probably set up an online course that you can take and learn exactly what you are looking for. And while you won't get 'credit' for it at some school, you'll learn it from someone who's actually doing it, and for way cheaper than you would if you were to go get a traditional college degree. Nowadays, for most things education, that's the way to go."

I sat for a moment preparing my next question, only to have that thrown to the wind by Dave's follow up.

"You know, this is a perfect transition to rule two," he said.

"Positive influences?" I replied. "Sounds like you needed some."

"Yeah, exactly. And thankfully, I had some. They just weren't strong enough in my life. But, it was looking back on what happened when I dropped out of school that led me to developing rule two."

"Okay, well, let's talk rule two then."

PEOPLE MATTER

"Before we talk rule two, let me tell you about Perry."

"Who's Perry?" I asked.

"Perry is my friend Mike's father, and he's a big part of what taught me rule two. When I dropped out of high school, he took me to task. He told me I needed to be in school. In his eyes, dropping out was stupid, and he really put a lot of effort into stopping me. While most of my friends were cheering me on, he was there, fighting to help me, despite the opposition. When I got older, and I looked back on life, I realized that it was the people like Perry who were working to make my life better. As a teenager, I thought my friends were looking out for me, when in reality, what they were doing was encouraging intellectual suicide. I had unhealthy influences in my life, and didn't even know it."

"Strong words," I said.

"Yeah, but that's what it was. If I had listened to him, I wouldn't have spent years smoking weed, chasing girls, and being an idiot. While it worked out, dropping out of high school was actually a pretty stupid thing, and, because of the influences surrounding me, it was easy. I lacked the strong positive influences I needed, and it cost me. But, on the upside, that was a big part of how I learned rule two, so that's good."

"We need positive influences," I replied.

"Yep, and I'll tell you something, if you want a good life,

you better surround yourself with them. As many of them as you can put to use."

I was taken back by Dave's choice of words, and when I paused to think about them, he noticed.

"Don't like the 'put to use' part?" he asked.

"No, it's not the idea," I replied, "it's just that 'as many as you can put to use' is a peculiar way to say it. Is that what you meant to say?"

"Absolutely," he replied. "Most people try to surround themselves with tons and tons of good people, which seems like the right thing to do, but it's actually a mistake. What you really want to do, is specialize."

"Like we talked about before. The whole, 'If you want to be a baker, surround yourself with bakers, not programmers stuff. Is that what you are talking about?"

"No," he replied. "That still applies, but that's not what I'm talking about here. I'm talking about how time itself is a restriction, and that when we talk about our influences, we have to keep that restriction in mind."

"I get that, time certainly can be a restriction in my life," I replied.

"And," he said, "because time is limited, we need to make sure that we don't try to take on too much. If we surround ourselves with 200 people who are all great, it won't work, even if they are all great in the specific area we want to be great in. Even though we would have access to tons of the 'right' people, we would never be able to develop relationships of quality. And it's the quality of relationships that create the scenarios which give us the opportunity to learn. When it comes to relationships, when possible, you should always target having several great ones; not tons of insignificant ones. That's why I said as many as you can put to use."

"Got it. That makes good sense," I replied.

It was 2pm, and, as it did every hour, on the hour, an alarm on Dave's phone began to ring.

"Homework time," I said.

Dave stood up from his chair, and made his way to the stair case in the foyer. 'Homework' is the term we use to talk about the training Dave is doing to regain his ability to walk. He has different exercises that he does, literally, every hour, on the hour. If he's awake, once an hour, he's training. It's simple stuff, and usually only takes a minute or so, but still, it's constant. It's also the reason that he's recovering so quickly, so, I am glad he's doing it.

A minute later, with his homework completed, Dave returned to the table. We continued,

◆◆◆

If you're curious, we recently created a YouTube channel to share some of Dave's training videos. Go to the link below if you'd like to see what 'homework' looks like for a man trying to learn how to run again. The link takes you to the first video, which starts with his run training. You can see the homework in video 2 if you are looking specifically for that (plus you get to see how huge his dog Onyx really is).

https://www.youtube.com/watch?v=jTkRkM8a76g&t

(Sorry for the complicated link…when the books launch date got jumped forward, the ability to make this an easy to type in link got sacrificed! Sorry!)

◆◆◆

"Yeah," he said, jumping in like we were never delayed, "and here's the other thing most people don't understand about time; they don't understand *why* time is limited. They are stuck thinking about time limits like the length of a meeting, or the hours in a day, or the years in a life; but there's more to it. When you forget about *what* the limits are, you can start to discover the *source* of the limits."

"The source?" I asked.

"Yeah. Time is limited, but it's limited by us. We do it. To ourselves. It's us who says that the meeting is going to be one hour, not two. We say that we will measure our accomplishments by the day, or the year, or whatever random timeframe we feel like choosing. Other than death, it's always people who limit time. We do it, and when you realize that, you can start taking advantage of that."

"Okay, I'm following. People create the time limits. How do we take advantage of it though?"

"It's actually pretty easy," he replied. "If we recognize that *people* limit time, we only need to look at why, and then we can put that knowledge to use."

As Dave and I sat talking about time limits, one of his contractors came into the dining room, hoping to pull Dave outside for a moment. He needed to discuss an issue that existed with one of Dave's gutters. Dave got up to talk with him, and apparently, work would have to wait; there were gutters to repair.

After a few minutes, Dave returned.

"Where were we?" he asked.

"You were talking about time limits, and how if we understand why it is that people limit their time, we can put that knowledge to use."

"Yeah, here's the deal. People limit time, because people are selfish. Even when we don't mean to be selfish, we are. And within limits, that's perfectly okay."

"Want to give me an example?" I asked.

"Sure, take yourself for example. You won't spend all day here with me just cranking out this book, because you have things that are more important to you. Rightly, you prioritize, which is something everybody should do. Today, seeing your family is more important to you than finishing this book. Some things are simply more important than others; and that's how we prioritize. That's a good thing, but, in order for us to prioritize, we have to limit our time."

The irony of this conversation taking place ten seconds after Dave had to step away to work with the contractor, was priceless.

"But," I said, "that's *why* we limit time. We were talking about using the knowledge of *how* people limit time. How do we do that? Specifically."

"Simple," he replied. "If I want to get more of your time, I need to figure out how to get higher up on your priority list."

"And, how do you do that?"

"Also simple," he replied. "I give you value."

"Value?" I asked.

"Yeah. The more valuable you see spending time with me, the more time you'll be willing to spend with me."

"I get that, but, how do you provide value?" I asked.

"That one, well, that one's not that simple. The short of it, is that everybody is different, and everybody is the same. Everybody has things they value, and that's step one. Find out what they value. Once you know the answer, if possible, provide it to them. To use you as an example, I know that you care about people. So, if I want more of your time, if I'm doing something that helps people, I know I'll get more of your time than if I just offer you a paycheck. Make sense?"

"And if you can't find that out?" I asked.

"Then provide generic value until you can. Take whatever you are good at, figure out how that could benefit them, and offer it to them. That would at least get a shoe in the door, and then grow from there. If you wanted to make more money, I can teach you that, and then you would want to spend more time with me. If you needed help shoveling your drive way, and it was worth it to me to develop the relationship, I can come by and help. There's a million ways to add value to people's lives, just find one of them, and then find a better one, and keep going."

"Okay," I said, "that makes sense. Let's go on then. We've covered surrounding ourselves with *specific* good influences, and that we need to manage our time with them. We've touched on how to improve relationships. But, we haven't addressed how to gather relationships yet."

"Or who to target," Dave replied.

"No, we did that. Bakers, not programmers."

"No," he replied, "that's the category of who to target. I'm talking about *who* you should target."

"As in, which particular baker?" I asked.

"Yeah."

"Okay, have at it."

Dave licked his lips like he was about to sink into a steak.

"This is the best," he said, "because it's the easiest. Are you ready?"

"Yeah, I'm ready. Let's hear it."

"Are you sure you're ready?"

"Yeah Dave, just tell me."

"Alright, here it is. All you have to do, is kill your ego, and then..."

In another attempt to build excitement, Dave added a dramatic pause.

"Dave, I'm writing, not buying, just tell me," I replied.

"Okay, but it's big. Here it is…"

Again, Dave paused. Because I know him, I knew what

was going on. He wasn't just selling, he was excited. Too excited. To him, it was so easy, and so good, that he couldn't just let it out there. He waited long enough to get me to make a face, and then he continued.

"You work the ladder," he said.
"The ladder?" I asked.
"Yeah, the ladder."

I asked him to explain what he meant, and his face lit up like mine does if you ask me to talk about my daughter.

"Happily," he replied. "It's like this. If you are standing in front of a 20ft ladder, unless you're giant, you can't touch the eighth rung. In life, there are people that will be just as far out of reach. At least, not at first. But, those people could help you, a ton, so, we have to ask ourselves an important question. What do you do, so that one day you can actually get to them?"

"I suppose you have something better than 'jumping' as an answer."

"Of course," he replied. "And again, it's easy, which is great. All you have to do, is target the people that you can reach, and then foster those relationships. You don't need to reach for the eighth rung. Just find somebody that's above you, and, if you are doing it even half-right, over time, they will help elevate you. Maybe you end up getting to the fourth rung. Maybe the fifth. It doesn't really matter, because even if you only get to the first, you can now reach the eighth. Make sense?"

"It does," I replied, "but, we probably need to explain the rungs to people."

I knew my question would serve to excite Dave even further, but I won't lie, watching him get more and more amped up was great fun for me.

"The rungs," he began, "are thought processes, and knowledge, and relationships. They are the secrets that you only learn once you've gotten there."

"The secrets?" I asked.

"Yeah. The secrets. It's like this. When I was young, I mowed lawns. I did some work, and I made some money. Because it was a lot of money to me at the time, I thought I was doing it right. I was on rung one. Eventually, I got older, and I understood the power of scale. You see, if I knew the power of scale when I was eight, I could have made a lot more money doing a lot less work. I would have hired a friend to do the work. I would have paid him $10/hour, which would have been huge for him, and I still would have made $15 for every hour of work. And the great part is that in this scenario, I'm being paid for work that I wouldn't have been doing. My buddy would be sitting there on rung one, happy as a clam, while I would be sitting there, also happy, but richer, on rung two. Each level up, is a little bit better thinking. A little bit better understanding."

"That doesn't seem all that secret," I replied.

"Sure, that might not seem like a secret," he said. "But I didn't know it when I was 8, and it cost me. And anything you don't know, is a secret you are yet to reveal."

"That might be why you didn't do it, but what about your friend? Maybe he already knew that, but didn't have a lawn mower. Or maybe it was just that he didn't know how to sell the service to your neighbors. Then he would have known it, and still not been able to take advantage of the knowledge," I replied. "What does that do to the idea of levels being about knowledge?"

"Nothing," he replied, "that's part of the levels. First off, if he didn't know how to sell the services, he wasn't on the same level. Second, if he didn't have the mower, he needs to save money while at level one, so that once he gets the knowledge, he can execute on it."

"How does he save if he's only making $10/hour?" I asked.

"We'll get to that later on; we need to stay focused on the levels for right now. What people need to remember, is that first, you get the knowledge, then you apply it, then, eventually, you get to progress. But, without the knowledge, you get nowhere. Using myself as an example, when I buy hundreds of homes at one time, it's because I know how to do it. Most people have absolutely no clue how to do that. It's beyond their level. But, I didn't get the knowledge and then just go do it. I still had to develop the capital to do so. I learned what I didn't know, sacrificed so that I could apply it later on, and leveled up."

David M. Prentice and Joshua M. Gordon

LEVELING UP

"Okay, let's say that Mark is trying to 'level up' as you called it. He meets Bob. Bob's a fifth rung type of thinker, and Mark is sitting at rung 2. What's next?"

"Beyond adding value to Bob's life?" Dave asked.

"Yeah."

"Listen, learn, and be humble," he replied. "There's no sense in pretending you are on their level, they already know that you aren't, so just be real."

"Anything else?" I asked. "Any particular strategies, tactics, methods? Something specific perhaps."

"Mark needs to not be afraid to ask," he replied. "If he's aware that Bob knows things that could help him, he needs to respect Bob's time, but he can't be afraid to ask him for help, particularly with knowledge. Fifth-Rung Bob has the ability to say no, so, Mark has to let him choose if he is going to exercise it or not."

"That's good," I replied.

"I know," he said.

Dave smiled, and I laughed. Onyx (the aforementioned Great Dane) just laid there like the 200 pound oaf that he is.

"Alright," I said. "Mark learns from Fifth-Rung Bob, and with his help, finds himself on the fifth rung right with him. What happens to the relationship after that?"

"The three relationship model," he replied.

◆ ◆ ◆

For the record, neither Dave nor I are the creators of this model. It's time tested, and well known in the psychology world. For those who haven't read it, here's the three relationships model made easy…

There are three relationship types:

1. You are teacher, they are student.
2. You are student, they are teacher.
3. Neither are student, neither are teacher, both parties are peers.

You should always try to have at least one of all three relationship types. There are reasons and times to have more of one type than the others, but at all times, try to have at least one of each.

◆ ◆ ◆

"Josh, you do see that we are actually a great example of the three relationships model, don't you?"

"Sure," I replied. "A weird one, but I see it."

"I mean think about it," he said, "because it's kind of crazy. I learned the three relationships model from you. Your thinking on that was at a higher level than mine was. You brought me up. And, crazy enough, I know things you don't know, so, when I can, I bring you up. It's textbook ladder work."

Dave's right. He and I really are textbook ladder work. Each of us has risen to top levels in our fields, and because of that, we can teach each other. And not only can we teach each other, but we also benefit each other because we both have access to people that the other person doesn't have access to. Which, really, means that we are in some way on two separate ladders, but working the other up their own ladder none-the-less.

"Let's get back to Fifth-Rung-Bob," I said. "You meet him, he is a good influence. Maybe he's a mentor. Maybe he's just a guy who does some things really right, and being around him helps you get those things right yourself. Once you get to rung five, like Bob, and now, you can reach Tom who is on rung 12, what happens to the relationship with Bob? You two are peers now. He's no longer the teacher/mentor. Beyond what you said earlier, what do you do with him?"

"He's your peer, so you treat him like one. The last thing anybody should do is to try to kick Bob off the ladder, or to step on Bob, or anything like that. Those are the moves of a fool. They are shortsighted. When we are sitting talking about relationships that help you grow, all I'm really saying is that if you want to be better, you need to spend time around people who are better than you. Bob might be great, but if he's not better than you, you won't be improving; so Bob's a peer, and you treat him like one."

"So," I replied, "you aren't eliminating Bob from your life, your just, what, reclassifying him?"

"Exactly," he replied. "Maybe it changes your conversations. Maybe it changes how you view your conversations. And, maybe it changes how much time you spend with them. If you are missing out on the time you need to foster the relationships that grow you, because you spend too much time with Bob, that's no good. That's you sitting there, stuck, in a Bob shaped rut. Looking like Onyx over there. Getting nowhere."

I stopped for a minute, thinking about an old friend who I had to detach from. Without going into a long story, he and I were close, but he was very toxic. We were like brothers, but he was constantly trying to destroy his own world, and mine with it. When I got married, I couldn't let it continue, and eventually, I had to disconnect. It was very sad, but very necessary.

"Okay, but what happens when you get to rung 15?" I asked. "If Bob hasn't progressed with you, you're out of his reach. The way you think, will likely no longer make sense to him. Is there a point where you and Bob just have to disconnect?"

"No, not at all," he replied, emphatically. "You never have to disconnect. You might have to reprioritize, you might not be able to spend as much time with him, but you don't have to disconnect. Besides, if you are growing, unfortunately, he will likely disconnect from you."

"Like rocket boosters," I replied.

Dave looked at me with a curious look.

"Rocket boosters, on a space ship," I said.

"I have no idea what you are talking about," he replied.

"When rockets take off, they have different stages. They use engines that are called boosters to get to a certain height, and eventually, the explosive bolts that are holding the boosters on, do what they are supposed to do, and explode, dropping those boosters off of the main rocket. The rocket keeps going, and the boosters just fall away. Bob is like a rocket booster, who blows up his own bolts."

"Sure," Dave replied, still looking at me funny. "Like rocket boosters. We'll go with that."

Before I could ask my next question, Dave began to laugh.

"How do you know about exploding bolts and rocket boosters?" he asked.

"I read about it."

"Exploding bolts?"

"Yeah," I replied, showing Dave that I too, can be simple.

"Well, anyways, it's not all that bad that Bob falls off. The sad part about life is that when people aren't willing to climb the ladder with you, they are almost always trying to hold you down. For some people, the last thing they want is for you to climb the ladder, because if you do, they either have to do it themselves, or worse, they have to face the fact that they aren't willing. And man, that has to suck."

"Funny, do you know why the rocket boosters detach?" I asked.

The funny look on Dave's face went away, and in its place was a look that I can only assume meant that he was incredibly riveted by my rocket conversation. Or, he was humoring me. Could have been either one.

"Having used up all their energy," I said, "the boosters are now officially dead weight. They do nothing to help the rocket climb, and while are attached, the weight they add makes it impossible for the rocket to ascend any further. They didn't have the energy to go any higher, and all they were going to do, was hold the rocket down, like Fifth-Rung-Bob."

Dave snickered a bit. I guess my rocket analogy worked.

"Fifth-Rung-Bob, the dead rocket," Dave replied.

"Yep."

"We've covered a lot here, maybe it would be good if you gave a short summary," I suggested.

"No problem," he said. "One, identify the type of people you should surround yourself with. Two, figure out who on your ladder you can reach. Three, figure out how to be valuable to them. Repeat. That's it. If you do those things right, everything else will work out on its own."

Like I said, when he wants to be, Dave can be a pretty simple guy.

"We never really covered non-business influences," I said.

"Well that's stupid of us," he replied, "That's probably the most important part."

♦ ♦ ♦

Dave's Challenge #2

Challenge #2 starts with identifying any 'level up' goal that you have. This can be personal, financial, educational, whatever, but if your 'level up' goal is for personal growth and not business, you may want to read the next chapter first, then come back here to do this. If business related, do this now, and then once you've finished, go ahead and move on to the next chapter to see how your personal relationships will impact your business life.

For those who are choosing right now to focus on a business goal, your job right now is to identify the single individual person who is highest up on whatever ladder you want to climb.

(as before and with all challenges, if you are reading this on an eBook, make sure you still write this down somewhere)

Once you've identified the person, write their name here

_____

Next, identify how they will help you level up. What will

you learn from spending time with them? Will you learn how to have a better marriage? Make more money? Live a happier life? Get a promotion? Have a better work/life balance? Whatever it is, write it here

_____
_____
_____
_____

With your person identified, figure out how you can add value to their life. Write it on the lines below

_____
_____
_____
_____

Almost done…

The last thing you need to do, is plan it. Look at your calendar, and dedicate time to building this highly important relationship. Once you've done that, write down when you will be getting together with that person here _____/_____/_____ at __:__ am/pm

Now, I know what you're thinking. "What if I can't connect to that person?" Good question, and the answer is Dave level simple; if you can't access your person, you screwed up step one. You are specifically supposed to identify someone that you *DO* have access to. We're not suggesting to call Richard Branson's assistant and ask him to dinner, we're only saying to reach out to the highest level person of which you *DO* have access to. As always, if you do the first part right, the rest of it works.

Now, go kick some tail and get started leveling up!

♦ ♦ ♦

Oh, and once you're done, don't forget to turn the page and read the next chapter, otherwise you're going to miss out on the personal relationships end of leveling up!

EVERY MOMENT COUNTS

With our everyday relationships at the forefront of his mind, Dave asked me if I remembered how his friends cheered him on for dropping out of high school.

"Sure," I replied.

"That's why it matters who you surround yourself with, far beyond just your business relationships."

"Makes sense," I replied.

"The crazy part is that most of the time, the problem with relationships really just fall into the whole dead weight thing. It's the friends who don't want to grow that you need to be careful about. Whether it's because they're scared to, or simply don't know how to, if someone doesn't want to grow, they probably don't want you to either. They'll weigh you down. That's why I said that the non-business relationships are more important than the business ones. They're too influential to be ignored."

"You really believe that?" I asked. "You really think that the social relationships are *more* important than the business ones?"

"Absolutely," he replied. "Imagine that you find an amazing mentor. He's a self-made billionaire who wants to help you build your business. Now, he's out for himself. He's helping you because he wants more money, and he's going to keep 10% of your company in exchange for scaling it huge. He has all the know-how, and enough incentive, but there is one problem. He's a level 138 thinker, and your friends are all at level 12. They all think you can do it without him. They all think he's ripping you off. And what do they do? They tell you how he's just coming in and preying on you. 'He's stealing your hard work,' they say. But that's because they don't know better. If you're operating at level 50, and that man can take you to 100, that's worth 10%. But you might not do it, because the people who are around you might go and convince you how foolish it is! That's why it matters."

Dave had gone into a full on teaching rant. It was fun.

He continued, "And you know, that's why you have to weigh out the advice that people give you. Look, all people are created equal. It's not that any one person is more valuable than another, but the advice of one person, it may be worth far more than the advice of your best friend Joey. And once you know that, you ought to be careful whose advice you are listening to. Never forget that. People are equal, opinions are not."

"I'm with you," I replied. "But I know for a lot of people, it's not easy to disregard the opinions of others. Why do you think that is?"

"Great question," Dave replied. "With an easy answer; they get selfish."

"We going to the respecter of persons thing?" I asked.

"Yeah, but you take this one," he replied.

"How deep do you want me to go?"

"Make sure they get it," he said. "They have to understand this, or they will never grow. It's an integral part of the secret sauce. They have to, have to, have to understand it."

"Alright, I can probably keep it to a page," I replied.

"No, give it ten," he said. "Give it 20 if it's needed. Don't let them miss it."

"Don't worry, I'll make it clear," I replied.

♦♦♦

Alright, I'm going to do my best to discuss what Dave is talking about, without taking three chapters to do it. I'm going to be as brief as possible, so here goes.

All of us, myself very much included, tend to be selfish in a peculiar way that we rarely recognize. What we do, is that we put the concerns of those we care about, over the concerns of other people. Allow me to give you an example to better explain.

> You, your child, and a random stranger, are stuck on a desert island. You have been there for 10 days, have no idea if you will be rescued, and have used up almost all of your food supplies. There is one bite left. Who's it going to?

Your answer is predictable, just like mine is. That food is going to you or your child, and that stranger is out of luck. That's how we operate, and we do it, out of selfishness.

I care more about my daughter than I do about that stranger or myself. If you have a child, you likely feel the exact same way. Now, I know what you are thinking. "I'm putting my daughter ahead of me, that's not selfish." You're wrong though. It is. Because the truth of the matter is that your child, my child, you, me, and that random stranger, are all human and all of equal value. We might not have the same bank account, we might not be of the same 'use' to each other, but in the big picture, my life, my daughter's life, and your life, are no more important than that random stranger's life.

107

When we put those we care about ahead of those we don't care about, we are being a 'respecter of persons'. We care about *who they are* in a way that is determined, really, by who they are *to us*. This is why it is selfish. I am happy if my daughter survives. *I* am the topic of that thought. When we realize that we think person A matters more than person B, and we think that because person A is more important to us, we are being a respecter of persons, and we are being selfish.

Without getting too deep into an ethics conversation, determining the value of a person based on their usefulness, is crap ethics. It leads to a pile of chaos and death, and personally, I do my best to never do it. I fail at it all the time, but I try.

◆◆◆

"Anything else on this one?" I asked. "The influences stuff?"

"Yeah, I've got one last thing," he said. "I want to drill down just a bit more on time limits."

"Alright, have at it," I replied.

"Okay, so, most people go through life without ever having a real awareness of death until they're very old. When I got my cancer diagnosis, I went from a 28 year old who thought I was invincible, to suddenly being aware that time is limited. It's one of the greatest gifts that cancer has given me, and now that I know it, there's no way for me to unknow it."

"That time is limited?" I asked.

"Yeah. In every sense of the word," he said, "and sometimes, it's more limited than we think. That means that every moment counts. And, I'll tell you this, if you think I'm going to spend my last moments with people who are going to drag me down, you've got another thing coming to you."

"That it?" I asked.

"It was it, but you asked, so, no. I want to give another quick summary, because I don't want people to miss this. I don't want people to be wasting their lives away because they didn't understand what we are talking about here."

"Okay," I replied, "then go right ahead and sum it up for us."

"Alright," he said. "First, surround yourself with positive influences, both business and personal. Pick the best ones you can get to, and make sure you work as hard as you can to grow those relationships. Second, grow, and if you pass up some people on the way, don't feel bad. If they leave you, that is on them. Be loving, and keep growing."

"Anything else?" I asked.

"Nope."

"Okay, let's talk about what happened after high school then."

David M. Prentice and Joshua M. Gordon

DOING IT ~~RIGHT~~ WRONG

"So, you dropped out of school, spent some time doing nothing, and eventually took some classes. Then what?"

"We got evicted," he replied, as matter-of-fact as if he was talking about a ham sandwich.

"Evicted?" I asked.

"When I was 17," he replied.

"That had to be an interesting experience."

"You know, for me, I didn't care too much. I was getting older, and it was pretty much time to get moving and be an adult anyways. My little brother on the other hand, it definitely sucked for him. He was seven. While the eviction might not have bothered me much, watching him suffer through becoming homeless, ugh, that hurt."

I asked Dave to clarify if he meant that it was hard for himself, or if it was hard for his brother.

"Both," he replied. "It sucked for me, and it sucked for him. And you know, he was innocent. He didn't do anything, and one day he's sitting there in his home, and the next day, it's just gone; taken from him. Even worse than that, it's not like you can teach him about mortgages, economics, business failures, or any of the other crap that went into that moment. All he knows is that he doesn't have a home anymore. That sucks."

For the first time in our interviews, I saw the hurt in Dave's eyes. When he was telling me about getting jumped by a group of guys in high school, it wasn't there. When he was telling me about getting diagnosed with cancer, it wasn't there. Even when he told me about losing his grandmother in a horrific accident, he still wasn't showing much emotion. But, when he sat there talking about his brother, and how he struggled, you could see it. It hurt. The real type of hurt. And it was obvious.

"After the eviction, where did you go?" I asked.

"After a little floundering, I got an apartment. My Dad got re-married, and moved in with his new wife Donna."

"Did you think about moving back to your mom's place?" I asked.

"For a second," he said, "maybe two. Not three though. She lives way out in the middle of nowhere, and like I said, it was time for me to be a man and make it on my own."

"Would you call that the start of your adulthood?"

"Yeah," he replied. "That day, I became a man. Whether I wanted to or not."

"And, how'd you do?"

"You know, I had gotten to the point where I understood a few things. I had seen enough to know both rule one, and rule two, real well. That meant that when it was time to take action, thankfully, I could. I didn't have all the tools, but I had two real good ones crammed up in my brain, and that was enough to be effective."

"By doing what?" I asked.

"I implemented the rules. Well, the two of them that I knew at the time."

"And when you did that, when you implemented the rules, what happened?"

"I knew exactly what I needed to do, and I did it. I

started a business that would help address the problem. I gathered a team of lawyers that could help people who were going to lose their homes. And that's exactly what we did, and it was awesome."

"What were the answers?" I asked.

"To the rules?" he replied.

"Yeah. If you knew rule one and rule two, let's talk about what your answers were. What mattered? What was your answer?"

"For me," he replied, "I didn't want to see little kids like Michael lose their home." (Michael is Dave's aforementioned younger brother). "If I could help prevent that from happening to some little kid, I had no problem working my tail off until all hours of the night. And, once I knew what I wanted, it was obvious that the next step was to figure out what the best way to do that was."

"And lawyers seemed like the answer?" I replied.

"Yeah. But only because I was a level six thinker."

"I assume you mean that as a bad thing."

"Yeah," he replied, "because I now know there are better ways. But, at that point in time, all I knew was what my father did when we were going through it."

"Which was?" I asked.

"In the road up to us getting evicted, my father dove deep into the legal system, doing everything he could to keep us from losing our house. For some time, it worked, and the way I saw it, the law was the way to go. The legal system was the way to stop kids from losing their homes. But, again, that was some low level thinking. Now, I know better."

"Is that why you changed industries?" I asked.

"That's exactly why."

I asked Dave if it was his answer to rule one that changed, or if it was just his approach.

"No," he replied, "the answer is still the same, I just learned that there were far better ways to keep kids in their homes."

"Like teaching people how to make money?" I asked.

"Yeah. You know, we were doing awesome things. We were helping people, and making money, which was great, but sometimes it just didn't matter. No matter what we did, in some cases, all we were really doing was delaying the inevitable."

Dave told me a story about a client that, in the interest of privacy, we'll use a fake name and call "Joe". Dave told me all about how Joe was this really nice guy. A hard worker, and a great dad, Joe was the definition of the type of guy David started his company to help. And, fortunately, Dave was able to help him; for a while.

Prior to employing Dave's company, Joe had gotten himself into a bad spot with his mortgage. He had missed several payments, and was about to lose his home. Dave's company worked with the mortgage provider, and got Joe's mortgage cut by almost 45%. Everybody was happy. The mortgage company was going to get paid instead of taking a loss, and "Joe" and his family would keep their home. It was win-win; except for one problem. The same bad habits that got Joe behind in his mortgage the first time, never got fixed, and six months later he found himself right back in the same bad position. In the end, all of Dave's work, was for naught.

"That's the problem we kept running into. We helped "Joe" get into a position where he should have been able to thrive, but he couldn't, because his mindset was wrong. He didn't know how to think like a rich man; he was too busy thinking low level. He figured he could skip a payment and play it out over and over again. He couldn't."

"So, your solution, really wasn't a solution."

"It wasn't," Dave replied. "Which, on first glance,

sucked."

"I take it by your words that there is a second glance that should be taken."

"Indeed," he replied. "Because, you see, it's stories like his that motivated me to start teaching people how to make money. That means that despite how ugly it was, good still came out of it."

"Is it working?" I asked.

"Like gangbusters," he replied. "As I said, rich people don't lose their homes."

David M. Prentice and Joshua M. Gordon

A QUICK GLIMPSE INTO DAVE'S CRAZY LIFE…

Before the chaos

Dave in the pits at a professional race, because, well, Dave, that's why.

With Richard Branson at the Detroit Tiger's game...
Then throwing out the first pitch.

Apparently, fear of heights is no problem for Dave…

Hold three grown adults on your back? Sure, why not?

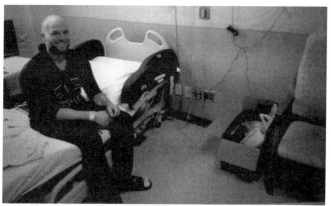

The first day I saw Dave at the hospital…a few days prior to his first brain surgery.

Him and Caren decided to do a photoshoot w/Onyx…just before brain surgery. "Because I live my life," he said.

Dave turned the hospital room into an office, again, because Dave.

Preparing…

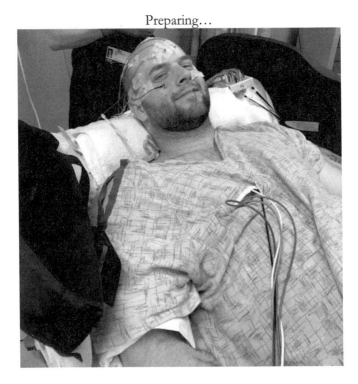

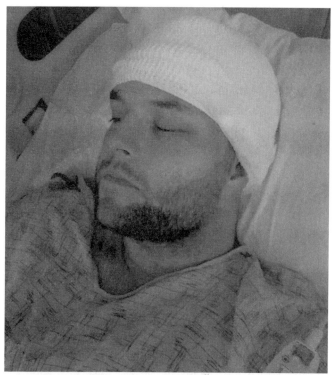

Post-surgery

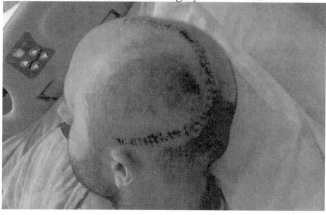

Head for the cure 2018

Head for the cure 2019

Onyx and Dave during one of our interviews

No joke, this photo has not been modified! That's what a 200lb Great Dane looks like on Caren (look at the next photo for some real context)!

FAILING IS WINNING

"What about rule three? When did setting goals become a rule?" I asked.

"When not having them nearly destroyed me," Dave responded.

"Woah," I replied. "Going to have to expand on that one."

"Alright, let me tell you a story. At one point in time, my brother Carl and I were business partners. Carl's a great guy. He's a really good person, and when we first partnered up, it seemed like it would be a great fit. A year into our partnership, he was still the same good guy that he was at the beginning, and that was the problem. I was growing, but he wasn't. Not in the business at least. It was like two motors that are supposed to work together, not working together. I was going one speed; he was going another. And he was going the exact speed we started out on, so it's not like he was the screw up. It was me who was screwing things up. I didn't pace with him. And I didn't set things up in the beginning to ensure that he would pace with me. Eventually, I was just moving at a pace that he couldn't keep up with, and I ended up having to buy him out, which put a monster strain on our relationship. We're good now, but that was hard. I had screwed up rule 3, and it nearly destroyed our relationship."

"Well, that's sad," I replied.

"It was. It sucked. I should have set a standard at the

beginning that we would grow at a certain pace. I didn't. If we had those goals in place, he would have hit them; I know it. It would have worked. But, I didn't, because I didn't know better. Now, I know better."

"Did you think that goals just didn't matter?" I asked.

"Kind of," he replied. "I used to think that hard work would get you where you wanted to go; that goals weren't really needed. That's crap though. Goals are like mile markers. If I'm in a race, and running my tail off, without mile markers, who knows where I might end up. Goal drift may drag me off to the side, and instead of getting where I want to be, I end up in Jersey. Nothing's wrong with Jersey, but if I'm trying to get to California, and I find myself in Jersey, I've screwed up."

"So goals, are your barriers," I said.

"Totally. They keep you on track."

I was just about to ask Dave if staying on track was a struggle for him, when, comically, his phone alarm went off. It was homework time once again.

Dave went into the kitchen, propped himself against the wall as he was supposed to, and performed 10 leg movements designed to help him learn how to run.

Once he finished them, he came back, and I asked him about struggling to stay on track.

"Staying on track has been a huge struggle for me," he replied, "and not just in my past. I still struggle with it to this day, but only if I screw up rule two."

"What happens if you screw up rule two?" I asked.

"I get pulled away," he replied. "I've trained the ability to stay focused, I'm good at it, but, if I don't control who I let around me, they'll pull me away from my goals, and I can't let that happen."

"Hence not screwing up rule two," I said.

"Yeah. Fact is most people are shortsighted and lazy.

Your goals scare them, so they'll tell you how your goals are crazy, out there, too much, too extreme. What they are really saying though, is that *your* goals are too much for *them*."

"And, does rule two solve that?" I asked.

"Most of the time," he replied. "Employees can be a challenge though."

"How so?"

"I've got this slew of people, and we work real hard to create 'buy-in'. When we hire people, we look for the kind of people who are interested in achieving the company's goals. When we do our job right, the employees play a part in achieving our goals, and we make sure that they understand that when the company wins, they will win. So, if I hire right, and manage right, employees are no issue. If I screw up anything in the process though, they can be a nightmare. They can real quickly pull you off the goals. Sometimes even when they are well intended. If their goal doesn't line up with the company goal, it's dangerous."

"That's a good bit of management, isn't it?"

"It is," he replied, "but success requires management. Businesses flex, every day. There's always something new, always something changing. If you can't flex with them, you fail."

"Does that mean goals flex?" I asked.

"It does. My company has a big-picture goal, and sub-goals. Each year we create a goal, and break that down into quarters. Quarter one, affects quarter two. Two affects three, etc. But, every business is different. Some will need more management, meaning more frequent goals, and some will need less management, meaning less frequent goals. Either way though, they better have goals."

♦ ♦ ♦

Many years ago, I worked for what was at the time a

billion plus dollar publicly traded company. This massive company had over a hundred locations, and 20K plus employees, and from what I could tell, maybe five of those employees liked working for them.

While I was on a vacation in Arizona, I ran into the CEO of the company at a gym, and the two of us ended up talking for almost an hour and a half. Over a smoothie, we had a surprisingly open conversation. He told me all about how the company grew faster than they could handle, and that the management of the company recognized all too well that there was a break in the management quality at the mid-level. In an attempt to address the issue, amongst other measures, they started implementing sales goals and metrics for every position that existed in the company. Even maintenance teams had goals. Sales teams would have weekly, and sometimes daily goals. They were trying to corral the sheep. They were trying to build the fences.

Unfortunately for them, while they tried, they never learned how to properly develop employee buy-in, and it didn't work out as well as anybody would have preferred. But that story is for another day.

◆◆◆

"For me," he continued, "there was a day where I realized that nobody will ever care as much as you will. Soon as I realized that, I decided that goals were going to have to be necessary. Achievement takes longer than a week, and that means that I have to keep people focused on the goal, or everything will go up in smoke."

"How complicated do you get?"

"I never get complicated. Not with goals. Or principles for that matter. Keep them simple, and clear, both for yourself and for others. If they aren't, you will never be able to act fast when decisions have to be made, and often, time is money."

"What do you do when you miss your goals?"

"That's assumptive," Dave replied. "Why would you think I ever miss my goals?"

"Because I know you. I've watched you do it a thousand times. You never set realistic goals, they're always through the roof crazy."

"That's true," he replied, "but that's because with myself I always apply the whole 'shoot for the moon' theory. But that's because of my personality. I win. With shooting for the moon, even if I lose, I win. For my team, when it comes to goal setting, we factor in the personality of those involved. If they're like me, yeah, sometimes the goals are so high that they might do their best, and legitimately miss them. If they aren't like me, and can't handle that type of thinking, well, I probably didn't hire that person."

♦ ♦ ♦

"Shoot for the moon. Even if you miss you'll land amongst the stars."

-Norman Vincent Peale

A relatively famous quote, this is Dave's approach to goals. The idea is somewhat self-explanatory, but just for the sake of clarification, here's how Dave puts it to work.

If his investment company bought and sold 500 houses last year, this year, he would assess the market, assess his current strategies, and barring any reason not to, he may decide to set the goal of buying 1,500 houses this year. Now, he may only hit 1000 houses, but he would much rather buy 1,000 houses and consider his goal missed, than to have a goal of 600 houses, hit it, but end up having bought 400 less.

He'd rather miss and be great, than hit and be less.

◆◆◆

I asked Dave what he meant by 'that type of thinking', and he told me about how he needs to have people on his team who can deal with failure. They have to be okay with missing. If they can't be okay with missing a goal, he can't be okay with them being on staff.

"We're hitting another dichotomy," I said. "You want to win, always, but you want your employees to be good with failing. Explain that."

"Failing is winning," he replied. "In fact, there's not a winner on Earth that isn't a failure. Michael Jordan lost hundreds of games. His loss record is something like 30 some-odd percent. That dude failed over and over again, and is one of, if not the best basketball players of all times. In 1997, Apple, what is now one of the biggest companies in the world, almost went bankrupt. The stories go on and on. People need to remember that failure is part of success. Those who aren't okay with failure, rarely succeed. Personally, I try to fail, and fail often. It's an indicator that you are pushing; that you are trying to grow. It's beautiful."

"Alright," I replied, "I'm assuming that you aren't talking about people *not* caring about their goals, but just that they are missing them. Yes?"

"Oh, yeah," he said, emphatically. "You better care. If you don't care, you screwed up back at rule one. Lazy doesn't succeed. What I'm talking about is going for the gold, laying it on the line, and knowing that if you fail, if you don't get gold but end up getting silver, well, it sucks that you didn't get the gold, but at least you're on the podium. But, to be ultra, ultra, clear, if you get silver this year, you better be aiming for gold again next year."

"I think we just covered rule five," I said.
"We did," he replied.

Dave's Challenge #3

It's time to set some goals. What we are doing here, right now, is just an exercise. While you should take the time to set goals for any and everything you care about (I even set them for improving my volume of family time), right now, we are simply going to focus on one goal.

Dave's Challenge #3 is to identify a learning goal. Pick something that if you were to learn about, it would improve your life. It could be something simple like wanting to learn how to change your oil so that you don't have to pay someone else to do it, or something highly complex like you want to get a Ph.D. in molecular biology. Whatever your learning goal is (and you need to have one),

Write it here

_____

Next, identify why. What will learning this do for you? How will it change your life? Write it here

_____
_____
_____
_____

Almost there...How you will learn it? Will you read a book (or 12)? Will you listen to a series of podcasts? Will you find a mentor? However you are going to achieve your learning goal, write it here

_____
_____
_____
_____

Last but not least, set a date for when you will have accomplished it. Goals without deadlines are wishes, don't just wish, do

___/___/____ at __:__ am/pm

Remember, this is an exercise to improve your life. Take it seriously, do it, and change your world for the better. Then, when you have time, start setting goals for the rest of your life. If something matters, give it a goal, and watch it improve!

This is another type of challenge that is great to proclaim to the world. Telling the world will force you to hold yourself accountable to your goal. Once again, share your goal with the #watchdavewin hashtag so everybody can root you on and help hold you accountable!

After mentioning that we had just covered rule five, I told Dave that we were out of order, and that we hadn't talked about courage and rule four yet.

"That's okay," he replied. "Until I got cancer, I knew something about courage, but nowhere near as much as I know now. For that reason alone it makes sense to me that we would just wait, and talk about rule four when we talk about the cancer stuff."

"Okay," I replied.

I glanced at my notes and realized that we still hadn't discussed David's rise to success; a seemingly important topic all things considered.

ONE DAY I'D BE RICH

"When was it that you actually became successful?" I asked.

"There was one particular day that, if you made me settle down on a certain point in time, was the moment I became successful; and I'll never forget it."

I asked Dave if it was the day he saw two different commas on his balance sheet, and he laughed and told me it was the opposite.

"Yeah, no. It's not that I had millions, my success came when I realized I didn't even have one comma yet alone two."

"What happened?" I asked.

"I was convinced by a loving third party that I needed to actually fill out a balance sheet on my life. I did it, and I was ashamed."

"Of what?" I asked.

"I had never done a balance sheet before. I had no clue how much of a screw up I was. When I first started it, I was all excited. I had $5,564 in the bank, and I remembered hearing once that the average American doesn't have even five grand in savings, so I thought I was awesome. Then I finished the sheet. When I did that, I realized that I also had $5500 in debt, which meant all I really had was $64. That sucked. Not only was I not 'great', I wasn't even average. I had no assets, which was pathetic, and that day I decided to change that."

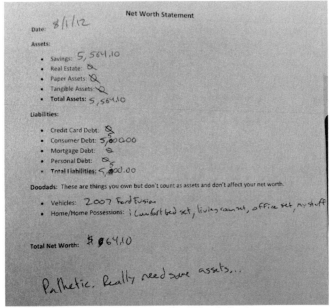

Dave's first ever Net Worth Statement

"This is the day you credit as the day you became successful?" I asked. "To be clear, what I was really asking was kind of when you 'made it', if you know what I mean."

"I know what you mean," he replied, "and this was the day. It's the day I started to do things right. It's the day when things began to grow. Every dollar amount, every growth metric, all of them, they are just products of the right mindset and the right actions. When I got those two things in order, I became successful."

"Okay," I replied. "Then, what did you do next? You realized you had no assets, and then what?"

"I paid off the debt. I had to. I was ashamed. It wasn't the smart way to do it, but I needed it."

"You needed it?" I asked.

"I don't know why, but I know that I needed to be out of debt. It wasn't an option. Not mentally at least."

"And you were what, 22 years old at the time?"

"Yeah," he replied, "but what does that matter?"

"Just getting a timeline in my head," I replied. "That's all. What happened after you paid off the debt?"

"Well, before that, I decided that I would never let myself be in that position again. I would never be the guy who let a lack of self-control dictate my life. So, after I paid off the debt, I started saving. The very next month I saved every penny I could, which was like $700. When you compare it to the $64 I had the month before, it was great. When I looked at my bank account and realized that I had increased my assets by almost 1100% in one month, I asked myself what would happen if I just kept doing it, and I realized the simple answer that one day I'd be rich. So I did. I kept at it. And it paid off."

I told Dave that for context, we needed to include what he was earning per month.

"Obviously, if you were making $20,000/month, that wouldn't have been too hard," I said.

"Yeah, and if I was making 20k each month then it would have been easy, but if I was, I would have saved way more than $700. Truth is I was making next to nothing. About $2k/month. I was poor. I didn't save money because I made a bunch, I saved money because I didn't spend it on anything other than what I had to. I was sharing an apartment, which kept my rent to about $300/month, and my car was cheap and paid off. I didn't go to the bar. I didn't take vacations. I didn't waste money on things that would only make me happy short term. And once I took the unnecessary things out of my life, it left enough for me to start saving."

"That's all pretty great," I replied, "but, you didn't get rich saving $700/month. When dd it go from saving, to what I can only assume was growing?"

Dave smiled at the question. We had hit another of his favorite topics.

"I saved properly, and constantly," he replied. "I never made the mistake of letting myself get 'rich' in my head. Over time, that way of living got me to the point where I could actually access investments. And then, the real money happened."

"How long did it take?"

"It was about four years before I could access truly good investments. I had made some stupid investments before that, primarily because they were good deals, but I was screwing up left and right on opportunity costs. If I knew then what I know now, I could have made a lot more money, a lot quicker. And easier."

Dave stopped talking about saving, and stood up to shake his legs out. Before our interview session, Dave had finished a session of recovery training that put a significant strain on his right leg. It was hurting him, I could tell. He wouldn't complain about it, but I could see it.

"You okay?"

"Yeah," he replied. "Sore, but that's okay. It's progress. I like progress."

After a few more moments of stretching, Dave came back to the table and we continued.

"Where were we?" he asked.

"You were telling me about when you had saved up enough money that you could start investing it."

"Right," he replied. "So yeah, first, some stupid investments, and then, my next screw up. More than once I made investments that were dependent on the economy.

Never do that; it's stupid. Thankfully, despite how stupid it was, thanks to pure dumb luck they ended up working out."

"Completely luck?" I asked.

"Oh yeah, I guarantee it," he said. "As far as those deals succeeding, I assure you, neither knowledge nor skill had anything to do with it. But, on the up side, with each deal, I got better. I learned what was an okay investment, and what was a great investment."

"Now, as a real estate investor, obviously most of your investments are in things like houses, apartment buildings, and things like that, but that isn't going to help most of the people reading this book. And, if we aren't helping people, that means we are forgetting rule one. How does this information play into the reader's life? When you teach people who either aren't in real estate, or don't yet have the assets to even look at the idea, what do you do with those people?"

"You're right, most of my assets are in real estate, but that's just because it's what I know. I know housing, so I invest in housing. If Bob knows cars, then, if there are good investments to be made, Bob can invest in cars. It doesn't matter what the investments are in, what matters is if the investments are good. That's it. What the reader needs to know is to stop wasting money, save as much as possible until they can put their money to work for themselves, and once they can, invest in what they know. One of the interesting parts of my life is that most of my investment strategies have changed drastically in the last four years. Originally, it was always about amassing a large fortune. First, I wanted to hit 100k in the bank, with no debt. Then it was a million. Eventually I realized that what I really wanted was freedom, and the real key to freedom isn't even assets, it's passive income. So now, most of my investments are in things designed to give me passive income, even if they don't create immediate and massive changes to my bank account. Again, as for the reader, they don't need to invest in real estate, they just need to invest in themselves by saving, and then one day putting their money to use, that's it."

When creating a plan for the book, I debated if readers would be interested in hearing about how Dave built his business. I asked him if he wanted to include it, and he told me that he felt like it didn't matter.

"If someone implements the rules," he said, "it works. No matter the industry, if they implement the rules, they can succeed. But to put the methods into this book, beyond the rules, that just wouldn't work. Each industry requires different things, not to mention how different everybody's goals are, so I don't think that how I did it, in my particular field, would be of any use to them. Remember, it doesn't matter how I coach an employee, or how I evaluate a volume-home purchase. What matters, is if I implemented the rules."

"Alright," I replied. "I get that, but, part of what you wanted to accomplish with this book was to help people thrive. And you wanted economics to be part of that. Can we end this just like that, just 'apply the rules', and leave it?"

"We can, because until we get to the specifics of a person's work, it's that simple. Stop wasting, save, invest. If they want more specific than that, they really are going to have to bring in a coach to give them guidance on it. It's just too diverse a thing to possibly fit into a book."

"Okay, that's where that ends then."

"Wait," he said, "make one of the challenges an asset sheet. It changed my life, and if they take it seriously, it might just change theirs."

"Okay," I said.

Dave's Challenge #4

Asset sheets. Nobody loves them but Dave and accountants, but he's right, they're valuable. It's impossible to know how to get to where you want to go, if you don't know where you are, so, with that in mind, here's Dave's Challenge #4.

There are plenty of versions of asset sheets; this is just an incredibly simple one to get you started. If you want to stop floundering in the wind, and know where you stand financially, take the time and fill out the numbers below

Date:
Assets:

- Savings:
- Real Estate:
- Paper Assets:
- Tangible Assets:
- Total:

Liabilities:

- Credit Card Debt:
- Consumer Debt:
- Mortgage Debt:
- Personal Debt:
- Total:

Total Net Worth (Assets – Liabilities):

To be clear, I wouldn't suggest sharing this with the whole world. Feel free to do so if you want to, but I assure you that it will likely introduce all sorts of ugly into your life, so I heavily suggest that you don't. For this challenge, instead of tagging #watchdavewin, maybe just post a cat video or something, and just kick butt on your own in private.

♦♦♦

"You know Dave, if we're following a chronology at all, which, I mean, we kind of are, we should probably touch on your second seizure and all of that."

"Oh joy," he replied, laughing. "We're going to need Caren for this."

GETTING HIT DOESN'T MEAN THE FIGHT IS OVER

To make this a little easier, here's a quick rehash of Dave's medical history up to mid-2019.

June 17, 2018, Dave had his first grand mal seizure. On June 26th, after 11 days in the hospital, brain surgery #1 takes place. Coming out of the surgery, beyond the extreme swelling and discomfort, Dave's function on his right side was severely impaired. Come July, Dave was able to begin his recovery training.

October 6, 2018, with his training going great, David hits a personal best 1017lb leg press, and everything is looking amazing. From that day, until June 2019, everything was going great.

"I was living like a monk," said Dave.

"A monk?" I asked.

"Yeah. I ate perfect, I drank perfect, I lived as close to perfect as any human being has ever done. And when I got my first MRI, it showed. Then, when I got my second MRI, it was even better. I was treating my body like I needed to, and I was doing great."

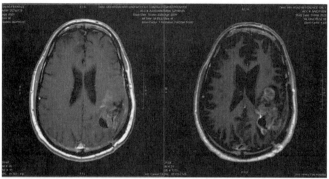

Dave's May 2020 MRI compared to his March 2020 MRI...at that point, everybody was happy, happy, happy!

I told Dave how I remembered being shocked at how well he was doing, and took a moment to compliment how clean he was living. The man was doing everything and anything he could do to better his chances, and it was pretty great to watch. I want to call it cool, but it just seems too disconnected. Awesome might be right.

"It seemed like the medication side-effects were the only thing bothering you," I said.

"Yeah, as far as things that were a problem, that was really it. I hated the meds I was on. I always felt foggy. Slow. Like somebody had control of my brain and turned me from a level eight to a level two. It was frustrating."

At that point, Dave's recovery was going great, but he was growing more and more frustrated with the side effects of his anti-seizure medication. Eventually, with the approval and guidance of his medical team, he attempted to wean off of them.

For this portion of the sit down, Dave's wife Caren was brought in to help with some of the details that we both knew Dave might not have.

"Thanks for helping," I said, prompting Caren to laugh at the idea that she possibly wouldn't.

"Of course," she replied.

"So, Dave, let's talk about your second grand mal seizure. You want to start, or should Caren?"

"Nah, let's let her have a go at it. I was out for most of it, and I was busy having a seizure, so, who knows if I'm even remembering it correct."

I looked over to Caren and asked her what it was like.

"Horrifying," she proclaimed.

As we normally did, we were sitting at the dining room table in the front room. I was at one end, Dave was at the seat next to me, and Caren was sitting opposite me at the other end of the table. Two computers and a pile of bills sat in between us, and just off to the side, sat Onyx (the giant Great Dane), and Kylie, a 30 some odd pound dog that looked like a chihuahua when standing next to Onyx. As was the pattern, I had a protein bar, and Dave and Caren had a great looking plate of food. A salad for Caren, more chicken and Brussel sprouts for Dave. Apparently, I needed to up my food game.

Onyx and Kylie living the rough life…Gotta love that his
leg is longer than her entire body!

"Horrifying is a pretty good choice of words," I replied.
"I've only seen a seizure once before, and I don't think I'll
ever forget it. I was volunteering in the nursery at church,
and a four year old boy had a seizure right there just a few
feet in front of me. Horrifying really is a pretty good term
for those moments."

"Yeah, if you've seen it, you know what I'm talking
about. It's scary," she replied.

"Did you have any idea it was going to happen?"

"No, and that was the worst part. Everything was going
so good, and it was just kind of out of nowhere."

For some time before Dave's first seizure, he was having
problems with his right hand. In a manner that appeared
completely random, Dave's hand would just go numb,
seemingly out of nowhere. He was suffering from
something called auras. In some people, they present like
they did with Dave, and in some people it will present
differently. Twitching is a common occurrence, but doesn't

146

always happen.

"Were you having any auras?" I asked.

"I did," he replied, "but I had been on anti-seizure meds for something like a year, and the auras were just an expected side-effect of getting off of them."

"Why didn't you get back on your meds?" I asked.

"I really thought it was just part of getting off the meds. I didn't know anything was wrong until the day I had the seizure. That morning, I was a little off. I kind of felt it coming. At that point, I did take the meds, but it was too late. They don't work instantly, not the ones I was taking at least."

"So, you knew it was going to happen?"

"I was worried about it in the morning, and when it was just about to happen, I was standing there in the kitchen ad I felt my hand start to go funny."

"Like with the first one," I said.

"Yeah, which was crap. I'm standing there in the kitchen, arm going funny, and I'm just flashing back to the first one, knowing I'm screwed."

"Maybe you should stay out of the kitchen," I said, failing to hold back my bad sense of humor.

Thankfully, everybody laughed.

♦♦♦

I have this horrible tendency to make jokes when things make me uncomfortable. Thankfully, Dave's got a great sense of humor. If it weren't for his ability to laugh at nearly anything, including himself, this process likely would have been quite somber. But, due to his odd mixture of confidence and humility, it was a lot of fun, and a lot of laughs.

♦♦♦

"Okay, so you are in the kitchen, your hand is feeling 'funny', and then what?"

"I'm sitting there on the couch," said Caren, "and he just walks up to me and taps me on the arm. He's looking at me and says 'seizure'. Next thing I know, he falls on the couch in a full on grand mal seizure. He's shaking all over the place, --"

Dave interjected to mention that he had 'pissed' himself during it.

"Wait, what?" I asked, trying to remember that Dave wetting himself isn't funny no matter how good our friendship is, at least, not if it's from a seizure.

"Yeah, I wet myself. And yeah, you can laugh," he said, knowing me all too well.

I couldn't help but to do so. I didn't want to laugh, but this is my buddy Dave. The millionaire who leg-presses a half a ton. The 'big-man'. And, he wet himself. It wasn't actually funny, but it's such a dichotomy, my brain couldn't do anything but laugh.

"I'm sorry. I really didn't mean to laugh," I said.

"No, it's cool. I know. Shows you how crazy bad a seizure can be."

"You're not kidding," I replied.

I had to take a moment to compose myself, and once I had, we were able to move on to what happened at the hospital.

Caren spoke up, "We get there, they pump him full of anti-seizure meds, and get him in for an emergency brain scan. They're trying to figure out what's going on, and I'm just sitting there, hoping to all high hopes that he's okay."

"And, how was the scan?" I asked.

"It was fine," she replied.

"No growth?"

"No," said Dave. "It really was just the fact that I had gone off the meds. My body just couldn't handle it."

"That had to be a relief," I replied.

"Kind of," he said. "Anti-seizure meds suck though. They're not as bad as cancer, but they still stuck."

I noticed that Dave mentioned cancer 'sucking'. I'm not sure if it actually was, but I think that was the first time that he treated it like it was a negative. Which is awfully crazy if you think about it.

"But, you know what," Dave continued, "I think that was the day that I really got to find out if I was courageous."

"Because it tested you?" I asked.

"Yeah," he replied, "and in a way that most people never get tested. When I got the first diagnosis, I really thought I would just beat it. It was like being in a boxing match, knowing you were going to win, but getting hit with a really hard jab in the first round. You don't think you're going to lose; you are more just surprised that he hit you with a good shot. But the second seizure was like getting knocked down in the championship rounds. You aren't out, but it matters. It means something. It tells you that you are in an actual fight, and all your confidence, all your 'knowing' that you are going to win, doesn't change that you are in a fight. When I got hit with that second seizure, I knew I was in a fight."

"And that tested your courage," I said.

"Like nothing else ever could have. And I'll tell you this, I've been through the ringer in my life. I've been poor, I've been homeless, I've been dumped, I've been pretty much everything you can be that makes people go 'aww, that's horrible', and all of it made me stronger. All of it prepared me for that one moment. I got tested, and I found out that I could respond. I was courageous. My training did prepare me. I was ready. And that's why I'm winning, because I've done the work."

For all the time we spent on David's youth, we obviously didn't cover everything. One of the pieces we skipped, was that at one point, he was a Golden Gloves winning boxer. Because of this, if you knew Dave personally, you would know how predictable his use of the fight analogy was.

Much of Dave's strength comes from the fact that he has faced challenge after challenge in his life. He's been beat up, and survived. He's been knocked down, and got back up again. It's this pattern, this repetition, that he credits with building him into the type of person that looks at a cancer diagnosis as nothing more than the next fight.

I hope you noticed how he responded to the challenge. It's one of Dave's best attributes. He never said the hits didn't hurt. They did, but he *chooses* to look at them as tests. That is why he is so successful. In his crazy mind, there is no challenge that is bad. It's a powerful thought, and his expertise at owning that idea is what's saving his life.

Dave, back when his arms were bigger than my head.

Dave's Challenge #5

This challenge is a little different. This, is simply about preparing.

The thing we are preparing for, is the battle. The battle that will come, unquestionably. While Dave's current battle is brain cancer, we all have a battle, and whatever yours is, courage will help.

The challenge with courage, is that it's more like a skill than it is a choice. It's something you practice, and get better at. In a way, it's the result of deciding to fight, and then progressively taking on bigger challenges.

Dave's challenge #5 is simply to decide to be courageous. That doesn't mean you need to go to war, or face your biggest fears (not yet at least), it just means that you need to decide that you will be courageous.

Once you've decided to be courageous, write it down

My name is _____, and I am courageous.

Next, build the skill of being courageous. Find something little. Whatever the smallest thing that you are scared of doing is, do it. Are you worried about asking that girl out on a date? Do it. Are you worried about asking your boss for a promotion? Do it. Find something little, that you can conquer, and do it.

"BUT, BUT, BUT!" you say. "What if she turns me down? What if the boss says no? What then?" It's simple, your goal right now isn't to succeed in that way. Your goal here is to simply do something you are afraid of so that you can build your ability to be courageous. If you are too scared to ask out the girl of your dreams, go find some random girl to ask out where you won't really care if she says yes or no.

BUILD THE ABILITY TO FACE FEAR AND DISCOMFORT

The truth is that with most things, we make big deals out of little things. If you don't get the promotion you are looking for, that's not an exclusively bad thing. It tells you where you stand with your employer, and once you know that, you can either figure out what you need to do to move up in the company, or, for that matter, if you should bother to stay! If your dream girl or boy shoots you down, you can find out why, and grow from it. Maybe he/she is horrible and you will learn that they are far from a dream, and closer to a nightmare. Or, maybe you will find out something about yourself and have the opportunity to become a better person. Whatever it is, don't let fear of loss dictate your life. Winners don't do that. Be a winner. Conquer your fears. That's challenge #5, and it's simple as doing it.

Now, back to seizure talk...

♦♦♦

Caren got up from the table, somehow aware that we had finished talking about the seizure. "Is that your rule four transition?" Caren asked, as she walked towards the kitchen.

Dave and I both laughed, appreciating that she was able to pick up on the pattern even though she wasn't in the room for most of the work.

"We already did rule four," I replied.
"Alright," she said, "well, have fun then boys."

Caren exited stage left (otherwise known as going upstairs), and Dave and I continued.

"Dave, tell me the truth. Was there really never a time where you thought you were going to die? Did you really think that you would just beat this, unquestionably, at every moment?"

"No," he replied. "There was a moment. It was about ten minutes long."

"Really, 10 minutes?" I asked.

"Yeah. I sat there, panicked, and prayed. Which was pitiful, because I don't really know how to do that."

"What did you do?"

"I started talking to God, but stopped because I felt disrespectful doing that in a crappy way. So I started sending emails to my work people, and started planning in case something went wrong."

"Fear, God, business continuity," I replied. "Probably not exactly the normal stages of grief, but that's not too surprising considering it's you that we are talking about."

"I know your being funny about it, but I don't think I was dealing with grief at all," he replied. "More than anything, it was kind of a moment of evaluation. For a second, I considered that I might die, and I didn't want the business to go under because I wasn't there. I had made some mistakes and my business was dependent on me, and I didn't want to be the lynch pin that broke my own company."

"You were trying to keep the mission alive," I said.

"I was. The last thing I wanted was to die and be like 'you did nothing worthwhile'. And, at the time, my business was the only worthwhile thing I was doing. If it had to be, I could die, but if my business were to die, I couldn't let it be due to my stupid lack of planning."

"I like that you felt the need to do something worthwhile," I replied, "but, why does that matter to you?"

Dave took a moment to reply. I assume he was trying to pick his words, but whether it was to be specific, or careful, I don't know.

Eventually, he spoke up.

"Josh, I don't have children. I have my wife, who's a grownup and handles her business. If I die, she'll be sad, but she'll be okay. I have my dogs, but they're fine and will be fine because Caren will take care of them. As far as doing something that matters, I have no one I need to raise up, and no one I need to take care of. The only thing that matters for someone like me, is that I did something for somebody."

"Which is great," I replied, "but sadly, I don't think that's how most people think. Not deep down at least."

"You don't think so?" he asked.

"No, I don't. I think it's common that people like the idea of helping others, but I think it's very rare that someone's last dying wish is to make sure that they are helping people. Where do you think you got that from?"

"First off, it isn't my last dying wish. It's simply my wish. Second off, as far as where I got it from, I have no idea."

"Maybe we will explore that more later, but for now, tell me about the time after the seizure. You got back on the meds, and then what? Things were okay, right?"

David M. Prentice and Joshua M. Gordon

PARADISE?

"Once I got back on the meds, things were going great. Life was going awesome, and if all I had to do was deal with the medication side-effects, okay, no big deal. As for the food, I was still eating and living really clean, so, once we got the meds situation handled, everything seemed like we were on track to easy street. In fact, life was so good that we planned a monstrous trip. It was going to be so epic that we were just stupid excited."

I had a question that I needed to ask, but as his friend, I really didn't want to. I waited, and decided to go an easier route for now.

"You're talking about the Europe/Africa trip, right?"

"That's the one," he said. "Forty days seeing the most amazing sights, eating the most amazing food, living the most amazing life, and all of it with my super-hot wife. Who could ask for anything more?"

"Man, who does that?" I responded, holding back a chuckle.

"People who can," he replied.

"What was the best part?"

"The lions. We saw lions. Like, real lions. In the wild, and I don't mean some animal park in Ohio where they can roam 50 acres. I mean the real, honest to goodness wild.

That was amazing."

Before I could ask a follow up, Dave continued talking. He was so excited to talk about his dream trip, that he couldn't wait for me to ask a question.

"But," he continued, "just as amazing as the lions, was the food. We went to some mind-blowing wineries, and some of the world's best restaurants. The only way I can describe it is to say that it was just out of this world awesome. Stupid expensive, but awesome."

"Which was better?" I asked.

"The lions," he replied, "because they didn't try to kill me."

"How did you handle work while out of the country like that? 40 days away, much of it without cell service or internet connection, how does that work?"

"Remember when I told you that I had made the mistake of making myself a lynchpin in my business, and that I needed to correct it?" he asked.

"I do."

"Well, I corrected it. Simple as that really. While I was away, my team handled everything, because I've done my job right."

"Oh," I replied, "well, that's awesome."

"Yeah, once I realize I've screwed something up, I fix it. That problem was handled far before the trip took place."

"Okay," I said, "well, you know that we aren't talking about the trip because it was wild and wonderful, right?"

"Of course not," he replied. "Besides, I know you don't really want to talk about the trip, you want to talk about why it ended early. I get it."

Dave was right. His 40 day trip, covering over 20,000

air miles, and costing more money than most people earn in a year, ended five days early. It's end was the product of seizures that had gotten so severe that Dave and Caren were forced to return home early.

"You're right," I replied. "Obviously we had to get there eventually, so let's talk about it. Tell me about when the symptoms first popped up."

"It wasn't until we were a few weeks in," he replied. "If you remember, before the trip, I was living super clean. Everything was clean. Perfectly. Even the post-seizure MRI had come back clean. In our eyes, we were good to go. Young, healthy, free. In the beginning of the trip, everything was good. I climbed a mountain. And I'm talking about a real mountain. And I was fine. But, we were doing what everyone does on vacation; eating like crap. I was eating all the foods you aren't supposed to eat, and drinking all the drinks you aren't supposed to drink."

The aforementioned mountain

Dave and Caren on top of the aforementioned mountain

I interrupted Dave to verify that he wasn't having any symptoms before the trip, to which he said there were 'none'.

He continued, "Anyways, I kept drinking too much, and then I felt like crap the next day. I just thought I was hung over, so I did the whole hair of the dog thing, and drank more. At first, it seemed to help, but towards the end of the trip, even when I was drinking less, it was just getting worse."

"Did you think it was the tumor?" I asked.

"I wasn't sure," he replied. "At first, I just assumed it was the food and alcohol. Then, when it was getting worse even though I wasn't drinking as much, that's when I started to wonder. By the end of it, I definitely had some fear running through my bones."

Caren had returned to the room, and kindly added some info.

"He was actually having seizures," she said. "Not grand mal, but seizures still. We were in South African wine country and he was in bed, shivering away like we were in the arctic. His teeth were chattering away while we were in 120 degree heat. It was crazy."

I asked Caren what she was thinking during all of it. "Did you think it was the tumor?"

"It was there," she replied. "It's always there. That fear. That it would come back. But, we were running from it. I don't think we wanted to face it. Eventually, we had to."

"What did you do?" I asked.

"We called his doctor, who told us about the dangers of all the alcohol intake, and that it was apparent that something was going on, but he wasn't freaked out. He didn't even tell us to come home."

Even knowing most of the story, I'll confess that I was pretty surprised that the doctor didn't tell them to come back right away. I asked them why they weren't concerned about him returning quicker, and Caren informed me that everybody was thinking it was likely post-seizure stuff, and there wasn't actually a reason to immediately assume that the tumor had returned.

"We missed his last MRI," said Caren. "Did he tell you that?"

We had not covered that.

"Yeah," Dave replied, "which was completely my fault. My MRI was late, and since I had been clear for all the other ones, I skipped the last one that I was supposed to do."

"Oh," I replied.

"Yeah," said Dave, "but based on what we know, it probably would have come back clean anyways. When this thing grows, I can feel it, and I felt nothing before the trip."

The 'thing' that Dave was referring to, is the brain tumor that he, Caren, and the doctors, are doing their best to manage. With a glioblastoma like Dave's, it is impossible for the doctors to remove all of the cancer with surgery, so they use a combination of efforts, including surgery, radiation, chemotherapy, and more, all with the goal of controlling it.

"When you guys came home, I imagine you went straight to the hospital to get checked out?"

"Pretty much," Dave replied.

"And that was New Year's Eve, right?"

"Yep. That's when they told me the tumor had grown, and that they wanted to cut my head open again and do another surgery."

"Happy new year," I said.

"Yeah, you might not want to spend holidays with me. Turns out I'm a real downer on holidays," he replied, once again giving us both a valuable laugh.

I DON'T NEED LIKELY,
I NEED POSSIBLE

"Surgery was January 3rd, yes?"

"Yep," he said.

"Same surgeon, right?"

"Yep again," he replied. "Same surgeon, same hospital, even the same scar. They went right back through the same spot."

"And, how'd it go?"

"Great," he replied. "Way better than the first time."

"Is there any reason?" I asked. "Do they know why it went so much better this time?"

"Who knows?" he replied. "My surgeon was awesome, but with things like this you never really know how someone is going to come out of it. Some people will go through the surgery, and be up and moving pretty quickly, others will be like I was and basically be a zombie for several days. When it was time for the second surgery, thankfully, I was on the better side of the results. Why that is though, who knows?"

"I don't imagine it has anything to do with mindset," I replied. "Not in the immediate, at least."

"It's a question of what you call immediate," he said. "The time period to consciousness, yeah, I don't think that has anything to do with mindset, but once you are able to start thinking, and pushing, and doing, then recovery is practically all mindset."

◆ ◆ ◆

Dave and I spoke in depth about the limits of what he is talking about. For the sake of space, I'm going to forego including the entire conversation, and just give a quick summary.

When people go through brain surgery, the outcomes are often unpredictable, and can vary widely. One person might come out, and be functioning great in a very short period of time. Another person might come out paralyzed.

When Dave talks about it being mindset, he is talking about the approach, not the case of results. Or the pace. Quite obviously, he is not suggesting that if a person comes out paralyzed, that their only issue is mindset. To be specific, he's saying that the rate at which they can recover, is heavily tied to how they approach the challenge.

And, for clarity, just in case anybody is thinking that Dave had an 'easy' time with this, when he came out of the surgery, his right side was not working. So, needless to say, he's got a pretty good understanding of what it's like to be paralyzed.

◆ ◆ ◆

"You ever heard of Hal Elrod?" Dave asked.

"The speaker?"

"Yeah, the Miracle Morning guy. Look at him. He's killed in a car crash, literally dead for something like six minutes, sits in a coma for a week, wakes up, is told he's screwed and that he will never walk again, and what does he do, he says screw that, and next thing you know the crazy man is running an ultra-marathon. From coma, to crippled, to running 52 miles straight because his mindset was right. It's mindset man. It's all mindset."

"Mindset, got it," I replied.

"And for anybody reading who might be in the same situation, put something in about how if they need motivation, all they need to do is to make sure that after the surgery they get placed in the neurology ICU. Do that, and you'll learn to walk real fast."

"Wait, what does the neurology ICU have to do with anything?" I asked.

"Because," he replied, "at least, at the hospital I was at, the neurology ICU is also where all the people with major mental issues were."

I asked Dave what mental health patients had to do with motivation for recovery, and he told me a story about how they were screaming and making noises all through the night, making sleep a near impossibility.

"You're laying there," he began, "your head literally just split open, brain played with, and sewed back together, and just trying to survive the ICU, and you've got all this non-stop noise. I was just thinking that I had to get out of there. Even if I had to fake it, it didn't matter, there was no way I was spending another night in that unit."

"What would you fake?" I asked.

"To get transferred from the ICU to a different floor, I had to be able to walk. I don't know how on Earth I would actually fake walking, but that's the point. I'm just saying that my mindset was determined. I was going to walk no matter what."

"I know it was several days the first time, how long was it before you could walk this time?"

"19 hours," he replied. "Well, 19 hours until I could kind of walk, at least. Enough that they were good with moving me to another unit."

"That was fast," I said.

"Yeah, I was actually out of the hospital four days after surgery, which is pretty amazing when you compare it to the first time."

"To say the least," I replied. "But, that's not the end of it. You went home, and then what?"

"And then it grew," he replied. "And man could I feel it. It was crazy. There were three weeks between the surgery and when I began radiation, and while the MRI's showed the growth, we didn't need it, I could have easily told them without them ever having to bother scanning me."

"What were you thinking? I mean, you're sitting there, you just went through your second surgery, you knew that you were going to have to go through additional treatments, but that had to be somewhat disheartening."

"I wasn't really focused on the change," he replied, "primarily because it was kind of expected. I mean, if it wasn't growing we might not have been planning the chemo and radiation and all of that, so that didn't really bother me much. I didn't like that I lost the ability to use a keyboard and mouse, that was annoying. But, primarily, I wasn't too focused on the tumor growth. Probably because I was too busy hating myself."

I've been close with Dave for something like a decade. We have both a work relationship, and a friendship. Even prior to this book, we knew each other decently well, but Dave's comment about hating himself for it came out of left field. Even though I spent hours a week with him, I had no clue that there was any point in time where Dave was blaming himself for what was happening; I was completely unaware.

"You hated yourself?" I asked.

"Oh yeah. I fed the beast man. I did everything I wasn't supposed to do. I ate tons of sugar, drank tons of alcohol, and just went to town being an idiot. I felt like I had done it to myself."

"You know that's not true though, right?" I asked.

"I do now, but it took a minute. I couldn't get past the fact that I skipped the October MRI. I kept replaying in my head that if I hadn't ignored the symptoms, I wouldn't have had to deal with this. But, eventually, something like three months later, I realized something. The MRI that I missed would have almost unquestionably come back clean. At that point, I had no symptoms. When the tumor was growing in January, there were symptoms; lots of them. So blaming myself over the missed MRI was stupid. And then, as far as the eating and drinking goes, while it was obviously stupid and something I shouldn't have done, I wasn't doing it in January and the tumor was still growing crazy fast, so it couldn't have just been me being an idiot that caused this."

"And when you realized that, you were okay? You stopped hating yourself?" I asked.

"Yeah," he replied. "Once I really looked at the data, I realized that I was being an emotional idiot, and I could let it go."

♦♦♦

December 27th, seven days before Dave would have his second brain surgery, unaware of what was happening in Africa, I messaged Dave to confirm an appointment we had scheduled for the next day. I wanted to make sure he had returned safely, and that we were still on track for our originally booked time. Obviously, we weren't. That was when he told me that they returned early due to medical issues. It's also when he told me that his car was stolen. What a week.

With our original appointment fallen through, David asked if we could get together the following Saturday instead. I said yes, and we were booked.

January 2nd, Dave sends a message telling me,

"I will be forced to cancel Saturday. Maybe

167

2 or 3 of them. Surgery on brain again tomorrow. Will keep you posted."

I was in the middle of a session with a different client, and I texted back that I would be calling him shortly. He told me that he may be in surgery prep, but if he wasn't, he'd answer.

When I called, he told me what was going on. That was when I found out his grade 2 astrocytoma had become a grade four glioblastoma. That is when I found out that his diagnosis was that he may die in "as little as three weeks, but who knows, could be a couple years."

As he was telling me about the diagnosis, he mentioned it with such little significance, it was as though we were discussing a grocery list.

> *"Yeah, pick me up some tomatoes would ya? Maybe some avocados? Oh, and I've got three weeks to live. Don't forget that we are low on bananas. Maybe we should get some just because."*

I forced him to come back to it, asking him if I heard him correctly. I had, whether I liked it or not.

While Dave was comparatively calm and collected about everything, I wasn't.

I'm a dad. Before I was a dad, I rarely ever cried. Not in my adult life, that is. But, since I became a Dad, I cry. Easily. Show me a movie where a little girl dies, and there is no question that my eyes will be wet. But, the only things I typically cry about, are super-family related things. Joy, fear, sadness, it doesn't matter, if there's tears, it's pretty much guaranteed it's family related.

When Dave and I got off the phone, I proceeded to spend the next ten minutes walking around the parking lot of my work, crying my eyes out. It was the type of tears I cried some 10 years prior when my grandfather had passed away. My friend was going to die, and I wasn't okay with it.

I walked around the parking lot, crying, praying, crying, praying, and doing my best to gain control of myself. I wasn't having all that much success, and it didn't help that I knew that I had only fifteen minutes before my next appointment would arrive.

I debated clearing my schedule and just going home. Just breathing, for a minute. Or an hour; or a day. I wasn't sure what to do, but I knew all I could do was pray, and let it go. So, I tried to.

I failed. I took my next appointment, and did my best to focus on the work so that I wouldn't be focused on what was happening. It worked, a little bit.

That night, I prayed. And, maybe sadly, I prayed harder over the coming weeks than I think I have ever prayed before. I prayed the types of prayers where you beg of God, then get mad at God, then bargain with God. I did all of them.

From the outside looking in, Dave was far calmer than I was. I doubt that's true, but that's how it looked to me.

◆◆◆

"I remember you talking about the first time," I said, "and how calm you were when they told you that you had a tumor. Was this one any different? Now that they had told you that you could be dead in the following three weeks, did that change anything?"

"It did," he replied. "They told me that with treatment, the average survival was something like 12-14 months. They said I 'might' make 10 months without treatments. And while there was some small part of me that was looking at this like 'holy crap I might actually die from this', there was still a bigger, stronger part of me that was down to fight."

"To survive," I said.

"If possible, but even if not, to at least enjoy the final months. Really, my first thought was the question of why I should bother with the treatments."

"Wait," I replied, "not like 'oh man I'm going to die', but, 'why bother with the treatments?' You were more focused on the length of life than you were the pending death?"

"It's tough to explain," he replied. "It's like there are two parts of you. One part has accepted that it could be a reality, so you better plan based on that, but the other part was like 'nah'."

"Nah that you wouldn't die?"

"Yeah," he replied. "My friend Theresa was given the same diagnosis last year, and died three months later, so I know it's real. But, I was always doing way better than they told me I was going to do. Every recovery, every detail, it was always better than what the doctors said it would be, so I didn't really think they were right."

Onyx stared at me with his head tilted to the side like he was waiting for me to say something profound. I had nothing.

Dave continued, "I think the thing with the treatments, was that it seemed like none of them worked. One of the doctors I was working with told me they only had five patients that had lived over 10 years. In my mind, there are people alive right now who were diagnosed with the exact same thing 20 plus years ago, but these guys can barely keep people alive to 10 years. If that was the case, the way I saw it, the treatments I was going to receive were probably the wrong ones."

"Is that when you started looking elsewhere?" I asked.

"Kind of, but not really. I had been researching this the entire time, but that was the point when I really kicked it into high gear. For months I had spent every bit of effort possible reading everything I could find on the subject. I talked with my surgeon, and he was willing to help arrange for me to see Dr. Friedman at Duke."

"The doctor you are with now," I said.

"Yeah," he replied.

"But what was the catalyst? What lead you to go somewhere else? Was it something you read? Something you learned? What?"

"I kept seeing accounts of people living far longer than they were 'supposed to'. The way I figured it, if pretty much everybody dies, but there is still some rare little remnant of people that are surviving, I wanted to find out why, and then do whatever it was that they were doing to survive. I decided that I would treat survival like I treat everything else; I don't need likely, I need possible."

David M. Prentice and Joshua M. Gordon

LIFE IS WORTH LIVING,
AND CAN BE LIVED

"What happened when you connected with Dr. Friedman?" I asked.

"Listen to what this guy did. I sent him all my stuff. The scans, the tests, all of it. And this big shot doctor who doesn't have to give a crap at all, calls me at like six at night. We both know he doesn't have to be doing that, but he did. And he did it before he ever received a dime from me. He just gave a crap. It was pretty cool to see."

"That's pretty great of him, but, what happened? He called, then what?"

"We set up for me to fly down to North Carolina to meet with him, which was good, because I was dying pretty quickly. My recovery was getting worse and worse. I was on tons of meds, and I really think that if I didn't see him and we didn't get a new plan together, that I would be dead right now."

"Wow. Those are some big words," I replied. "Do you really mean that?"

"Completely," he said. "Just look at what happened when I got down there. I'm lucky I even got to see him."

♦♦♦

Dave and Caren flew down to North Carolina to meet with Dr. Friedman, and their flight was anything but smooth. Part way into it, midair, Dave began having symptoms that would only worsen. By the time they landed in North Carolina, Dave was in trouble. By seven pm, use of Dave's right side was completely gone. No function; nothing. Dave would later tell me that he was so messed up that he couldn't even think, and knew he couldn't think. I asked him about ten different ways what on Earth he meant by that, and he couldn't explain it; which should give you a good idea of how bad things were. An ambulance ride brought Dave to the ER at Duke Hospital, where he was treated with a variety of medications. Twenty-four hours later, Dave had gone from completely paralyzed on one side and feeling horrible, to walking, talking, thinking, and feeling great.

♦ ♦ ♦

"Now, when you finally sat down with Dr. Friedman, what happened?"

"He had a plan," Dave said, "and it made sense. He told me that there was no reason I had to die from this. And you know what, that's what I want anybody reading this to realize. There is a way you can do it. There are people who have lived for 15, 20, nearly 30 years. Survivors. Which means that it can be done, despite what I was originally told. For me, that was everything. It kept me from being like **** it. People need to do the research, do the reading. When you find out about these people, you will quickly see that there are ways to make your probabilities better."

I sat silent, appreciating Dave's grit.

"You know, the people who get told they have terminal cancer, they have these thoughts that go ringing through their head. They ask themselves if they should bother, they wonder why there is no hope. I know that I personally was super pissed, and really just wished somebody would have lied to me and been like 'yeah, you'll do great, no sweat.' At least then I would have had some hope. Them basically telling me that there was no point in trying was nearly a death sentence for me. Thankfully, I'm too stubborn to listen, and found someone who could not only provide hope, but the care and treatment that I needed to get better."

"Thankfully," I replied.

We spent a few minutes once again talking about mindset, and how he felt that the original hospital he was at was just rampant with helplessness and despair.

"There were too many people around me just waiting for me to die," he said.

The fact that they called his tumor 'the terminator' told Dave all he needed to know; particularly, that these people had a mindset that he wasn't looking for, and didn't think would work.

Dave's got a simple mantra, that in a certain way is the basis for rule #2; don't mess up your mind. It was that mindset that led him to Duke, and to be willing to do anything he had to do in order to get the best care possible.

"The cost was going to have to be whatever," he said. "Out of network, traveling to North Carolina, the hotels, the rental cars, the fees, it didn't matter. If I was going to survive, it was going to require a team that wanted to work to see me live."

"How much was the first surgery?" I asked.

"Something like $170,000.00," he replied.

"Good thing you've got some money."

"No," he said, "good thing I've got good people, because it wasn't my money that made this possible, it was the people around me."

"Are you talking about the 'Let's Save Dave' campaign?" I asked.

"That's exactly what I'm talking about."

Note to the reader: To fill you in, when it became clear that the bills were going to add up to outrageous numbers, a good friend of David's set up a fundraising campaign called 'Let's Save Dave'. He created an online donation center, helped organize fundraising dinners, bowling events, and more, all with the goal of helping to pay for the insanely costly process that Dave was going through.

"Good thing you had surrounded yourself with good people," I replied. "Go rule two."

"Seriously. If I didn't have good people around me, my stupid self would have probably just sat there and let the bills rack up."

♦ ♦ ♦

What Dave wouldn't tell you, but I will, is that he fought the idea of anyone doing a fundraising campaign for him. In the beginning, he didn't want it to be done. He talked about how he doesn't need it, and how he can earn the money to pay for it, regardless of if it is millions of dollars. "I can make it work," he said.

Unfortunately, Dave was ignoring some simple realities. He might have millions in assets, but he also lives by his motto that 'cash is trash', and keeps most of his money invested in some way, shape, or form. So, while he had some cash for emergencies, it wasn't several million dollars. All of this was made worse by the fact that while he could turn his non-liquid assets into liquid funds, doing so would have meant divesting from projects midway through, which would have been extremely costly. And, none of that mentions the extreme risk he would be putting his wife into should something go wrong with the cancer. The idea that Dave could have just paid it off one day, is ideal, but unfortunately, none of us actually know what his future will hold.

A long conversation took place, and after a while, the people around him were able to convince him that if other people want to bless him, there is nothing bad about that, and he should let them. If he felt an obligation to reciprocate, when all was said and done, he could easily pay them back as funds become available. Or, he could do what they really would prefer him to do, and pay it forward.

◆◆◆

"And then what?" I asked. "Chemo, radiation, all of that, right?"

"I had already done the radiation," he replied. "Dr. Friedman recommended a drug that he wanted me on, which I took the very next day, and it was amazing. I went from being in the emergency room the day before, incapable of even talking, to perfectly fine the very next day. In 24 hours, I was walking, talking, and feeling great."

"Was that it? The new drug, and then you went home?"

"No, that wasn't it, that was just the real stand-out thing. There was a ton more. We went through the list of supplements I was on, and he told me which ones he thought I should remove, and which ones he thought would be okay to stay on. After the experience I had the first 24 hours there, I knew I had to listen to him."

"Can we talk about the treatment plan?" I asked.

"Sure, but I want to talk about Rosemary first."

"That's the nurse who works with Dr. Friedman, right?"

"Yeah," he replied. "She's amazing. She's open, and honest, which is so refreshing. It was really helpful to just have somebody who would shoot straight with me. I can't tell you how much I appreciated it. So, shout out to Rosemary, thanks for being awesome. If you're reading this,

I hope you know you change people's worlds."

"And, the treatment plan?"

"They said I was going to have 1 year of dealing with this every month. The Avastin (one of Dave's medications) every two weeks, 5 days of chemo, and 23 days of no chemo. We are on month six right now."

Note to the reader: This conversation took place in June of 2020

"Those first 24 hours in North Carolina, going from paralysis to jumping up and down, was that all you needed to see so that you could know that they had the right plan, or was there more to it?"

"There were three things that made me know I was at the right place. First, they made a plan, and then told me that if what we are planning to do doesn't work, they had other methods that we could look at. Second, they told me that there's a big difference between what you can do, and what you should do. They were happy to encourage me to push. They affirmed that there was no reason that I was automatically a useless person just destined for death. If I wanted to work, they were encouraging it. They encouraged me to exercise and be active. They wanted me to fight for my survival, which is awesome."

Dave paused; I think to enjoy the moment. I mentioned that once again he only had told me two out of three things, and he continued.

"You know they were calling me at 7:30pm. They got there early in the morning, and they are sitting there, calling me, checking on me, at 7:30 in the freaking night. How awesome is that? They're right along-side of me, joining in on the fight. I just can't really get over that. But I know, you asked for the third thing, and I still haven't answered that. Here's number three; they flat out told me, that while

I might die in the next year, that's not the whole story. They told me that it is possible that I can live far longer. Dr. Friedman looked me in the eyes, and told me that there's no reason I have to die this year. That was so refreshing. As tough as I am, I needed that. It gave me hope. It gave me the will to fight."

"That's great," I replied. "I remember how you came back a seemingly different person. You've always been pretty positive, but it did seem like you had a little extra pep in your step when you got back."

"Yeah, because the way I see it, the longer I live, the greater my potential to keep living. Medicine advances, science advances. If I keep fighting, my chances only improve. That's when I decided I was going to learn to walk again. And use my arm again. I figured, if I've got a chance, I've got to get healthy again. They gave me the reality that life is worth living, and can be lived. And while life will never be perfect, it can always be better, so I'm going to work to make it the best possible."

"That's awesome," I replied.

"It is awesome, and it's also what I needed. That was part of the problem at the previous place. Originally, nobody talked about that. Instead of encouraging me to fight, they were offering me wheel chairs even when I didn't need it. They were trying to be nice, but I didn't want to be coddled, I needed to be set free to fight."

Earlier, I mentioned that I had a question for Dave that I was avoiding. It was time though. Dave's feet were going to have to be put to the fire, even if I dreaded doing so.

"Dave, I don't want to ask you this, but I have to. Let's play a hypothetical. 12 months from now, if you're dead, what do you think about all this effort you're putting into your recovery?"

"I don't think there's a single chance that will be the

case," he replied.

"Can I push on you to pretend for half a second, and tell me what you think if you're wrong?"

"I factored that in," he replied. "I thought about my wife and what happens if I die tomorrow. I thought about my family and my business. I've done things to protect them. That's why I let the #letssavedave campaign go through, to protect her in case I'm wrong. I made sure that Caren knows what to do, and how to thrive if I'm dead. But I'm not wrong."

"I'm with you, but you still haven't answered me," I said.

"Okay," he replied. "As far as how I'll feel about all of it, I don't know, I've just never given it an option to be thought about. Not the way you're asking at least. If it ends up a 'waste', so what? Plus, look at life. I'm way lesser physically and mentally than I've ever been before, but I'm way happier. This book for example. This matters. The fact that someone might get something out of this, that's practically everything to me. If it changes people's lives for the better, even if it's in a little way, it's monster and worth all of it. So if I'm dead in 12 months, which isn't happening, yeah, it'll still all be worth it. But, I'm not dying, it's that simple."

◆◆◆

Dave spent some time talking about his wife, and how when the COVID-19 pandemic destroyed the industry she works in, she was able to pivot and create an entirely new business model, allowing her business to survive in a time when most of her competitors were having to close up shop.

I think, and I can only say that I think, it was Dave's way of showing me that he wasn't being foolish, that he knew what he was up against, that he really understood the odds, and he was planning accordingly. We spoke for some time about how he was very careful to ensure that if he should die, she knew how to handle his businesses and investments, and wouldn't get taken by anybody in the process.

At several points, I have debated if Dave was simply in denial. I wondered to myself if Dave's fight was really just his way of avoiding the reality of the situation. That's why I didn't want to ask that question. If it was denial, it broke my heart to think that I could possibly ruin it. But, after this conversation, I came to the conclusion that I don't think Dave's in denial. That's not what he's doing. He's got an outlook. He lives it, and moves forward, and I don't think there is a better way possible.

◆ ◆ ◆

Dave continued, "One more thing on Dr. Friedman. Besides the fact that he's one of the smartest people in the world, he was amazing because of his outlook. Here he is working a job where on a regular basis he has to tell people that they have terminal cancer, and he was peaceful, and happy. He told me he expects to see me for a long time. That outlook was astonishing."

"I'm getting a much better idea of why you are so fond of the guy," I replied.

Dave asked if we could move off of the treatment stuff, and talk about what he's learned since the diagnosis.

"You don't think people would be interested in the treatment portion?" I asked.

"No, not really," he replied. "I mean, some people, but probably just out of curiosity. But it doesn't matter. It's almost guaranteed that my treatments will be different from some other survivor's treatments. They need to figure that one out through research and time with the best doctors; not me. I want to focus on turning them into survivors, and if we talk about what I've learned, we can do that. Let's do that."

"Okay, let's do that. Let's talk becoming a survivor."

"THEY'RE JUST PROBLEMS, WAITING TO BE SOLVED"

Dave was excited.

Talking about survival brought out a side of Dave that would best be described as something primal. Passionate and angry might be close seconds, but primal seems to be the most accurate.

"Cancer was amazing for me," he said. "It changed my mentality in such a great way. It set me free. I've learned to be honest, no matter what. I finally realized how to just not give a crap about what anybody else thinks or does. I no longer care about my 'image', which is amazing, and I've finally figured out how to slow down. And sure, it was a bit by force, but that's okay, it's still great."

Dave's excitement was carrying him, and I started to see a smile cracking out of his typically serious face.

"You know what I do every morning?" he asked.
"I imagine plenty of things," I replied.
"Every morning, every single morning, I actually stop and talk to my wife. And I love it, and I would have never done that in the past."
"Really?" I replied. "Never?"
"Really. I was too busy. She was too busy. We love

each other, but we were too busy taking over the world to stop and look at each other in the morning. But cancer slowed me down, and man was it for the better. I had no clue on how much I was missing out on."

Dave didn't know she was there, but in the kitchen, well within earshot, Caren was getting some food together, smiling.

"You know what else is awesome?" he continued, "Sometimes, I can't speak, at all. There are certain words that when I try to say them, I just can't. I sound like a complete and total moron. And you know what, when my speech gets broken, I don't care. At all. It doesn't affect me in the slightest, which is crazy. Think about it, I speak professionally, and get stuck on my words some times; and I don't care! And neither do any of the clients, because I still get the job done. I win, even if it has to be a different way than I used to. Cancer may have given me some limits that I didn't have before, but all it has been able to do is change *how* I do things, not *if* I do them."

As Dave sat there, talking about how there is nothing he cannot do, I struggled with the question of if I should, or should not point out the fact that Dave suffers from a myriad of physical limitations, which means there probably are some things he can't actually do, even in a different way. The last thing I really wanted to do, was to point this out to him. His positivity is valuable, and I certainly didn't want to crush it. But, I know Dave, and I know he likes to live in reality. And, if Dave's not scared to be challenged, I figured I ought to do my job and challenge him.

"You know Dave, I love the attitude, but, do you think you're being realistic?"

"Absolutely," he replied. "Name one thing I can't do now that I could do before."

"Run," I replied, all too aware of how cold I was being.

"That's low level thinking Josh. You're beyond that. Running is just a form of transportation. And speaking of transportation, I can't drive either. But, the goal of transportation is to get from one place to another. I can take a taxi, use a car service, ask a friend, or whatever, but I can get from place A to place B with no problem. And, if you want to call running exercise, I might not be able to run for exercise yet, but I can exercise other ways. Remember, I said that it gave me limits, but didn't stop me. The method, running, and the goal, transportation and or exercise, are different. In the question of 'can I do it', I care about the goal, not the method. Besides, in a month, I'll be running."

◆◆◆

Note to the reader: He was right. One month after this interview, he was running. He had gone from being incapable of walking properly, to walking clean, all within a month, and did hit his goal of being able to run within two months. It was insanely fast, and an amazing example of what can happen when you join together determination, the right knowledge, and the will to do a ton of work.

◆◆◆

"I get it," I replied, happy to see that he was sitting firmly in reality.

"Yeah, there's no denial going on here. The doctors might have thought there was, but nah. I know what reality is, I just choose to look at it from the right side."

"I'm with you," I said. "Let's get back to what you were talking about in regard to cancer setting you free."

"It really did," he replied, "and it sucks that most people will never get to feel it. The joy of emotional freedom is the best high you can ever have. It's amazing, and definitely the second best thing that cancer brought to my life."

Surprised to hear him call it the 'second best thing', I asked him what was first.

"Gratitude," he replied.
"Gratitude?" I asked.
"I was an ungrateful *****. I put my happiness above my wife's. I put it above yours. I put it above everybody's. I was selfish, but now, I actually care about things like whether or not my wife is happy. I really appreciate these things that in the past just didn't matter to me."
"That's a good thing," I replied.

"Do you remember telling me that being generous pays off?" he asked.
"I do."
"Well, I always thought you meant in business, and money, but just in things like that. Never once did I stop to think about how much being generous in life, pays off in life. Take Caren for example. With her, I used to be inconsiderate, and now, I'm considerate, or, at least, better at being considerate. I'm working on it. And to no surprise, while she's always been considerate, now, she's even more considerate. She's always been, but it's been amplified. Like, at night, she turns the light off for me. That might sound like nothing to you, but it's huge to me. When I try to walk in the dark, it's pretty much guaranteed that I will smack my leg on something. Her turning the light out means I don't have to get all busted up by the bedrails. The fact that she even sees it is just awesome. And, in some way, I know it's partially because I've gotten better at being generous in life. It's paying off, and that's pretty cool. It's crazy that it was cancer that taught me all of that."

♦ ♦ ♦

Note to the reader: Just to add a little clarification, at the point in time when this interview was going on, Dave was still learning to walk again. Most of the time, his right leg would swing out to the right as he stepped, sometimes half a foot or more. This meant that when walking by a bed, or a table, or a chair, or anything of that sort, he was highly likely to kick it. Should he do that in the dark, he was also highly likely to fall, dangerously.

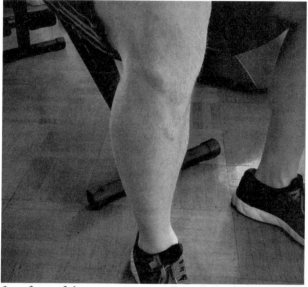

Just four of the many scars on Dave's leg from walking into things.

♦♦♦

"Dave, you really do ride an interesting dichotomy. You started an entire business with the primary goal of helping people. I know for a fact that you've lost out on lots of financial opportunities, all in the name of helping people. But here you are saying that you cared about yourself above all else. That statement doesn't really line up with what I know about you. It seems like a bit of a contradiction."

Dave paused for a moment, staring into space as he thought about what I said.

"It is," he replied.
"Then, how do you make sense of that?" I asked.

Dave waited a good 10 seconds before answering.

"I had almost zero empathy," he said. "Despite my experiences, I didn't seem to care about anyone else's. I think life had just kicked my ***. I was homeless. I lost my first love. She left because I was a screwup, because I was toxic. I think I was just burnt out, emotionally."

"But that doesn't address the dichotomy," I replied. "That would address you being a jerk, but there's still the part of you that was actively dedicating your life to helping people."

"Yeah, it's weird," he replied.

For the first time in our interviews, it became apparent that Dave didn't know why he was thinking what he was thinking. Dave is a man of systems, and in this case, we were talking about emotions, and feelings, not systems.

"I would do things to help people, but only in a statistical type of way," he replied.

"Statistical?" I asked.

"Yeah. There was no humanity in the way I thought. It was purely about a result. It was math, unless it was personal. If it didn't have a face, it was easy to be considerate."

"That's pretty backwards," I replied. "Usually people are considerate when it is personal, and inconsiderate when it isn't. Are you saying you were the reverse?"

"That's exactly what I'm saying," he replied. "I think I

was so burnt out, so destroyed, you know, emotionally, that if anything was personal, I had my guard up. I couldn't be considerate, because if I was, we could end up close, and I could end up hurt, and I was done being hurt."

"But you still wanted to help people."

"I did, and I suppose that's why I did it through things like my business. If I helped a thousand people stay in their home, I could help people, but they could never get close to me. I was some guy in an office. I couldn't get hurt in an office."

Our interview paused while we talked about how nice it was to be able to speak so openly about life. To share emotions with such brutal honesty was refreshing for both of us.

Dave asked me if he had told me about the Lyft driver. It was a story I hadn't heard. I'm glad he shared it.

"Alright, this is a good one," he said. "So, just after the second surgery, I had to go back to the hospital, but Caren was supposed to be working. No problem, I'll get a ride. This woman picks me up, and sees me all messed up. Bandages all over the place, walking all screwed up, barely able to speak properly. So, she's being super nice, showing me a bunch of pity, and asks me if I'm okay. I tell her 'yeah, I'm good, it's just cancer, no big deal'. She smiles and asks me why I was so positive, so I told her the truth."

Dave paused to build suspense, as he likes to do.

"Which was?" I asked.

"That my life is probably better than hers."

I spent a solid moment laughing, knowing all too well that Dave wasn't making this up. This is him to a tee, which is part of what I love about the guy.

"Yeah," he continued, "I told her that while I didn't mean it to be offensive, when I look at my life, and I look at what I have to assume her life is like, particularly when considering that she was working that job, my life is probably better than hers."

"What did she say?" I asked.

"She loved it. I was real friendly about it. I wasn't being a jerk; I was just telling her the truth. I listed out all the good things in my life, and pointed out the fact that outside of this one thing, everything else is awesome. Most people have some money issues, some relationship issues, some this issue, some that issue, but all I have is cancer. I told her that we both have problems, but mine aren't all that bad."

◆◆◆

Dave does this. He rides this psychological razors edge between reality and insanity. He looks at terminal cancer, he looks at past business failures, he looks at poverty, and all he sees are challenges. He's not unaware of what he's facing, he just chooses to see them in a certain way. It's great.

◆◆◆

"She wasn't upset?" I asked.

"No. She really appreciated the perspective. We talked some more and I told her that the way I see it, life has problems, and sometimes they have to be solved. What those problems are, doesn't really matter, they're just problems waiting to be solved."

"That sounds good," I said, "but, I'm not sure it really fits reality. I mean, I think of traffic as a problem, but I'm pretty sure that it's not on par with cancer."

"I agree," he replied. "Traffic is way worse."

We laughed for a minute, and then Dave went on to explain himself.

"It's like this. Some problems are big, some problems are little, but every problem that needs to be handled, needs to be handled. Once something falls into that category, the 'needs to be handled' category, that's what it is. End of story. Sure, some are more important than others, but if they are both in the same category, then they are both in the same category! Again, I'm not talking importance, I'm talking categories. Look at you for example. When you had the whole ant thing happen, you came over here all excited. Like, how crazy is it that you find out that carpenter ants are attacking your home, and you might have tens of thousands of dollars of damage, and you were happy about it. You weren't moaning about the cost; you were just excited that you found it and you were going to be able to keep your family safe and stop it from becoming worse. If you want to talk about positive mindsets, that's what we should talk about. And you know what, do me a favor and put that in the book. Tell people that story, because that's why I like you."

"You want me to put the ant story in the book?" I asked.

"Yeah, because seriously, that's really the biggest reason why I like you. That's how I try to be. It's the best way in the world to live life. When you can find the good in bad situations, you can be joyful no matter what. Why wouldn't you want that? We have to make sure that the readers know that."

◆◆◆

Well, here you go, the carpenter ant story, by request of Dave...

During the COVID-19 lockdowns, everybody and their mother was doing house projects, and my wife and I were no different. A little paint here, a little trim molding there, and all was well until my wife wanted to redo our fireplace.

Our fireplace has an exposed stove pipe that was previously maroon in color. Somebody loved it, but us, not so much. With the maroon stovepipe, there was a trim molding that was designed to complement it. At least, in theory. It was six inches tall, sat halfway up the wall, and stretched the entire length of the room. It was painted black, purple, pink, and gray. Again, somebody loved it, but us, not so much.

When we finished the fireplace remodel, riding the inertia that comes with completing a project, I grabbed a pry bar and started removing the aforementioned trim molding. Once it was off, we found water and ant damage, along with what had to be ten bazillion (roughly) carpenter ants. And the skeleton of a dead frog. No joke.

The damage was behind drywall, and we didn't know if we were going to be hit with a few hundred dollars of work and an exterminator bill, or tens of thousands of dollars and months of headaches. What we did know, was that if we hadn't found it then, it would have been worse later.

Sure, part of me was super annoyed. Part of me was concerned that it was going to be a ton of money. But a bigger part of me, the smarter part of my heart, was really happy to have found it. Had we not, it could have been much worse. We could have found it by a wall falling in and killing my daughter, and that would have been pretty horrible. So, with that in mind, while it appeared bad, finding it was good, and that's what I chose to focus on.

After ensuring that I included the ant story, Dave continued,

"I will say though, I do still get pissed about stupid stuff all the time. Traffic really does kill me. Traffic pisses me off worse than cancer. It's crazy."

"Is that it?" I asked. "Is there anything else you want to say?"

"Yeah, there is," he replied. "You know, I don't think people know what it's like to be told you have a year to live. You learn to really appreciate the things that matter. The people that matter. All the sudden, how you're going to spend your time is something you really pay attention to. With that flowing through my head, naturally, there came a point where I started to think about what really matters. Like, what truly, truly matters. I thought about all the little things; money, homes, travel. It took maybe a second to realize how limited all of those things were; how little they actually mattered. And it was sad, because I realized that if you were to look at my life before this, most of the stuff I worked hard to do, none of it mattered. When you face the idea that one year from now you're supposed to be dead, everything changes. Now, I'm not worried about real estate deals. Nor am I worried about big trips or special events. It's the things that actually matter, like getting this book done and out there so it can actually help people. Right now, this is the number one thing. I have to help people."

There was one last question that I knew I would eventually have to ask, no matter how much I didn't want to. It was a question that no matter which way Dave answered, I didn't want to hear it. But, it had to be asked.

"Dave, if God offered to take it all away, but doing so meant that you would lose all of these lessons, everything that you call 'good' that came about through this experience, do you do it?"

Dave thought about it for a moment. As he sat there,

eyes once again pointed to the ceiling, I dreaded his answer. If he says yes, then I have to question how honest he is being with himself when he talks about being so grateful for what has happened. If he says no, then I have to accept that he is willing to die for those lessons, and I don't want my friend dead. Either answer makes me want to puke.

"No," he replied, "I care about life now more than I ever have. Before, as much as I like to think I did, I didn't really care about helping people. And I really like that now, I care. In this new life, I've found something I can't replace. You know, I would trade everything I have for time with my wife. Before, I didn't think, feel, or act that way. I talk to my Dad every day now. I see my sister. Before, I didn't do those things. I had riches, but I didn't know any of the truly glorious things in life. So, no, I wouldn't reverse it, the lessons, and all that they've brought into my world, are simply worth too much."

◆ ◆ ◆

The best, and worst part of the question, was that simple fact that there was no 'right' answer. I will say though, as much as I didn't expect to, and as much as I don't like that I did, I did like Dave's answer.

◆ ◆ ◆

"You know what," he said, "there's this small percentage of the world who's interested in fighting, and needs the help. I want to help those people. There's underdogs who can make it, if they can only get the knowledge of what to do. That's who I want to help. If I die helping them, that's just fine. It's cool."

"I don't want you to die," I replied, "but, when that day does come, God willing 70 years from now, if you die helping them, I agree, that's pretty cool."

THERE HAS TO BE MORE

"You know, we've covered a lot, but I'm questioning if we've actually taught people how to go from being a patient to a survivor."

"We did," Dave replied, "just indirectly."

"Well, let's be direct. What exactly do you think someone needs to do?"

"That's simple," he replied. "If someone wants to be a survivor, all they need to do, is choose to live."

"Dave, I don't think it's actually that simple."

"Sure it is," he replied. "And, of the two of us, I'm the only one whose had to face down a terminal cancer diagnosis, so, I'm right on this one."

As funny as his comment was, I still had to press him.

"Alright," I said, "but jokes aside, that's not actually enough. I'm all for positivity, but, sadly, there's still plenty of people who go into these types of challenges with a positive mindset, and still die."

"Oh, Josh, you got confused. I'm not actually talking about not dying. We are all going to die one day, that's a given. It's the only thing more guaranteed than taxes. What I'm talking about is making sure that we are living, before we die. I'm talking about enjoying every moment. Being

195

able to suffer, and still love life. I'm talking about that wonderful sanity that is required to see something good in a bad situation. Survivors, are people who choose to live, while they can."

I noticed that Dave had called it sanity, and asked if he had meant to say 'insanity'. He clarified that he hadn't misspoken.

"Look at the ant thing. You get it. You saw a huge freaking problem, and saw how good it was that you found it. That's sane. It's insane to spend your whole life wallowing over the fact that there are problems, when everybody knows that life is going to have problems. Look, something will happen today, to both of us, and it will be a problem. The sane thing to do, will be to face it, and do our best to solve it. To do otherwise, now that would be insane."

Dave was in full on *DAVE MODE!™* (and no, there is no actual trade mark on *DAVE MODE*, I'm just being silly). He was talking as fast as his lips could move, and he was excited in a way that is all too rare. The truth is, from what I can tell, there really isn't much that Dave is passionate about, but, when we get into the topics that ignite his fire, man does he get going.

"So being a survivor, is about living life, while it's possible," I replied.

"And fighting," he said. "And I don't mean fighting death. Some people won't want to fight death, and while that isn't me, that might be somebody else. If you are 103 years old, have lived life, and just want a good final six months, cool. But be a survivor in those six months. Find out how to enjoy them. See the people you love. If you don't love anybody, go find people to love. Help people. You'll never know how amazing life is until you start helping people. Whatever the goal is, fight for it. If you don't want to die, look for every resource that exists. If your doctor doesn't have any treatments left to help you, search for other doctors. I did, and I thank God I did. When I was told I had a glioblastoma, there was a big enough part of me that was like 'I'm not going to die from this'. And while most doctors would just tell you that you are screwed, there are a small number of doctors that disagree, and I'm with them. And, so far, I'm right."

"Fight," I replied.

"Yes, fight. Hard. Whatever it is that you call 'living', fight for it. That's survival, and that's what I want people to know that they can do."

I asked Dave if there was anything else that he wanted to talk about, specifically about cancer, and he said there was, but he wanted to save it for the end. "It's the most important part," he said. "It should go at the end."

"That works," I replied, "particularly because we still haven't covered rule six yet."

"And what a perfect intro," Dave replied. "We are talking about fighting, and what better thing to fight for than freedom?"

Ignoring the fact that I had a potentially better thing to fight for, we continued.

"Rule six is fun," he said. "Getting free, is fun. Most will never do it, but for those who do, man are they in for a ride."

"What exactly does it mean though? When you say to get free, what are you talking about getting free from?"

"Good question," he replied. "We are talking about freedom from the restrictions that don't need to exist. We are talking about mental freedom, economic freedom, emotional freedom, all of it."

"Wait, is this a rule, or a result?" I asked.

"It's both. Getting free is the result of doing particular things, in particular manners. It is also the rule, that you must. My approach to life is this, figure out what matters, surround yourself with good influences, set goals, be courageous, fail properly, and get free. Get free is a requirement. It's an all-encompassing task that I have to accomplish. If I'm applying the rules to life, it's a big conversation. If I'm applying it to business, maybe it's as simple as getting my business to the point that it operates without me being there 24/7. If I'm applying it to my relationships, maybe it means that we get to the point where we know that all problems can and will be handled. Whatever we are talking about, the reason it's a rule, is because it's necessary."

"Why?" I asked.

"Are you asking why it's necessary?" he replied.

"Yes. Why does somebody *have* to drive for freedom? What if somebody doesn't want to?"

"Then they skipped rule four," he said.

I asked Dave why he thought a person must have skipped the 'be courageous' portion, simply because they aren't concerned about rule six, and he told me that since everybody wants freedom, the only reason they would skip it, was if they lacked the courage to take the risks necessary to achieve a life of freedom.

"Look, for most people, freedom is scary. If you're the boss, you're free, but it's all on you. You have no one to blame when crap goes wrong. In fact, I can't think of a single thing where adding freedom, doesn't add danger, at least on the surface. And it's scary, I get it. But, that means that somebody skipped rule four, and this is why rule four comes before rule six!"

"Do you think that people need freedom in *all* ways, or just in a few particular ones?" I asked.

"Personally," he replied, "I think they need it in all ways. If Bob feels free economically, but is an emotional wreck because he hasn't learned how to have a good relationship with his wife, life will still be a mess. Besides, it's not like you have to get them all correct at the same time. People can work on them one by one; I sure do."

"If they were to do that, to work on the different parts of life one by one, do you have an order you recommend? Should they take care of family first, then health, then money? Should it be A, B, C?" I asked.

"There's a 'best' order for everybody, but it's unique to each person," he replied. "Some people need to fix their economics before they will be mentally stable to fix their relationships. Some people need to fix their physical health before they will be able to fix their economics. Everybody is different, but everybody has an order that will be best for their unique situation. Helping people know the exact order they need to use would require far more than a book. That's where coaching comes in. That's where courses come in. Crap, that's half of why programs like those even exist, because they have to be customized. Unfortunately, books can't do that."

"Anything else?" I asked.

"Yeah. I don't want people to think I'm talking about money. Not exclusively at least. Because that's what it used to be about, but not anymore. Like the fact that cancer changed how I view family, and time, and so many other things, it definitely changed how I view wealth. It showed me that money isn't the dictating factor of a good life. Yeah, you need a certain amount of it, but, I assure you, as somebody with a lot of it, you reach a certain point where it just stops changing things. If you have a decent car, a nicer one won't really do much for you. If you have a decent home, the joy of a nicer one won't last all that long, or do all that much for you either. Take my house for example. It won't really change my life. If I sell it, or keep it, nothing will change. Not really at least. But, there are things in my life that seem little, that are far more important. The thirty seconds I spend with Caren every morning are worth worlds more than this stupid house. Sitting with her in the evening, I'll trade my fancy cars for that time all day long. I used to drive a stupid expensive luxury vehicle that cost more each month than most people's mortgage payment, but now I can't drive, and to most people, it's a loss, but it has meant that I now eat breakfast and dinner with my wife almost every night. Before all of this, if we didn't have a date scheduled, she never saw me before 8 at night. Now, well, now we are doing it right."

◆ ◆ ◆

As Dave fondly went on about his wife, Onyx looked at me with great confusion, and Caren sat there, once again smiling away.

And I have to tell you, this couple, they warm my heart. To see them go into this fight, together, loving each other, smiling, it's just a great sight to see.

They've got a funny relationship. They communicate in their own unique way; the product of two strong willed people who have decided to join together and fight everything and anything that they have to. When she's not around, Dave babbles on about how great she is. When she talks about him, she talks about how amazing he is. They're not perfect, and they'll be the first ones to tell you, but their unified, that's for sure.

If you were outside that dining room window, looking in on the three of us talking, seeing us laughing, you would probably think that we were busy reliving comical stories from our past. You definitely wouldn't know what was really happening. You wouldn't see Caren's fear that she is going to lose the man she loves. You wouldn't see my fear that "Dave The Unstoppable" might end up stoppable. And most likely, you wouldn't realize that what we were really doing, was everything we could to make every moment amazing. We all knew, despite our refusal to accept it, that those very moments, may have a time limit on them. We had to laugh. We had to cry. We had to be loving, because we don't know if we'll be able to tomorrow.

Well, at least, I think that's how Caren and I feel, Dave is probably just having a good time, because he wins. That's what he does. That jerk is expecting to be having laughs at the table 50 years from now; and thank God.

◆ ◆ ◆

Dave continued,

"I know I'm wealthy, like, financially wealthy, but I don't care. All the things that make me feel wealthy, none of them cost anything. It's not the house, the cars, the fancy dinners, the big trips, none of it. All the stuff that matters, they're all free."

"I agree, but it's kind of a funny thing to hear from the guy who wrote a book for people, specifically to help them get rich," I replied.

"I know," he said, "believe me, I know. But that's why I want to say this. It's nice being rich. Just because it doesn't matter, doesn't mean it isn't nice. And sometimes, I guess it does matter, like with the ability to access care that other people can't get to. Things like the best trainers, the best staff, all that takes money, so don't think I'm saying people shouldn't get rich, they should. I just want them to keep perspective on it. Money can be good, but it can't be everything."

"Which is what many people make it out to be," I

replied.

"Which is illogical. Think about it. There is only so much money that a person can make, and only so much stuff they can do with it. Money can't buy everything, and since it can't, there has to be more. There has to be something bigger."

"I agree. What's bigger for you though?" I asked.

"Helping people. That's definitely way bigger than money."

"Pretty honorable," I replied. "But tell me, how'd you come to that conclusion?"

"Because helping people makes me feel a million times better than making money."

As always, Dave was keeping it simple.

"To me," he continued, "wealth isn't just money. I mean, I know in a way that's what it actually means, but it's not how I think about it. To me, it's about who you become far more than what you get. My life is so much more enjoyable now that I know how to appreciate things, and care about things."

"I feel like I've asked you this question several times, but I feel it needs to be asked once again. How much do you think your viewpoint is impacted by the fact that you do have a good amount of money? I mean, it's not like you are talking about money like it doesn't matter from the position of not having it; you do have it."

"I have it now, but not before. While I didn't know how beneficial it would be at the time, both of my businesses were started with the question of 'what can I do for people?' When everything was based on that, I liked it, even when I was only making 20k a year. That's why I can confidently say that my thinking isn't rooted just in the fact that I don't have money problems; because it was true even when I did have money problems. It was true when I had credit card debt, it was true when I was homeless, and it's still true now that I'm rich. Look, it's definitely easier with money, and my money gives me options, but it was my mindset that gave me my money."

Throughout our relationship, I've watched Dave grow and change in remarkable ways. I remember when he first met his then girlfriend, now wife, Caren, and him racking up three thousand dollars in credit card debt taking her to fancy restaurants and buying her high priced bottles of wine. I think he kicked himself about ten thousand times when he told her that he was in debt and couldn't keep that up, and she was totally cool with it and didn't care. She was happy with a cheap sandwich, because she was looking for real happiness, not the type of smiles that money can temporarily purchase.

"When Caren and I first met, there was no reason to think I would make anything of myself. I was a high-school dropout, in debt, and had a business that I liked because it helped people, but made next to nothing money wise. Fast forward a few years, and look at my life after realizing how to live it right, and here we are eating and doing whatever we want. Now, I work a lot less, and make a lot more, but the view on wealth, that it's more than money, has been a constant. The only difference there, is that now, I have money."

"Dave, for a lot of people, particularly those who don't have money, that's a big difference. What happened to cause the switch? As I understand it, it's when you started your investment firm that things really changed, what led to that?"

"Rule one," he replied. "I stopped, and looked, and realized that I wasn't paying attention to what matters, so I changed it. Just because it was good, doesn't mean it was the right answer. When I figured out the right answer, and then put the rest of the rules to work, then, and really only then, everything clicked."

Dave's Challenge #6

It's been 54 pages since a challenge, I'll bet you thought they were over! But no, there's just one more.

Ask yourself this question,

"What do I want to be free from?"

Write it down here_____

You may have several answers, and that's great. Whatever you just wrote down, go back to rule #1, and see how they fit together. If you wrote down 'being poor', but your answer to rule one was 'family', then you now know that you need to figure out how to stop being poor, so that you can spend more time with your family. Whatever you wrote down, look at your answers, see how they apply, and take ownership of your life, now.

LIFE

"I want to talk about winning again."

"Okay," I replied. "What about it?"

"My entire life, I've wanted to win. Even as a small child, winning was the most important thing. Tic-tac-toe, video games, sports, it didn't matter; winning was everything. When all I cared about was keeping people in their homes, winning meant doing that, even if it meant I made less money. Eventually, I realized that I can win, help people, and be rich, all at the same time."

"Is that what drives you to still work hard?" I asked.

"In a way, but it's a little more than that. There's two things. One, tons of people came in and helped me when I needed help, and while none of them want money back or anything like that, I have to pay it forward. The way I see it, if people gave me a dollar, I better pay it forward ten-fold; so I have to work. Second, I like winning, and for me, making money is about winning."

"Like that guy who crashed the stock market back in 2010," I replied.

"Just like that guy, but, you know, without the criminal part. But it's a great example. I mean, look at that guy. He was a self-made multi-millionaire, and he was living in his parents basement. All he cared about was winning. It was all a contest to him, and if he didn't break the law in the process of the fight, he'd still be winning today."

♦♦♦

The man Dave and I are talking about is Navinder Singh Sarao. On May 6, 2010, Navinder executed a series of illegal stock trades that triggered a stock market crash that resulted in widespread economic panic. In minutes, companies lost billions of dollars, and consumer confidence that our economic systems were stable, and unrigged, went straight into the toilet.

While Navinder had earned roughly $70,000,000.00 (yes, 70 million dollars) trading in the years prior to that day, he still lived in his parent's basement, often ate at McDonalds, frequently utilizing coupons to save money, and never bought a single thing more expensive than the second hand Volkswagen that he bought for under ten grand.

The investigators found that Navinder, who both the prosecutors and defense attorneys described as autistic, saw trading as though it was a video game, and that he wasn't acquiring money, but points. He didn't care about the money, he cared about winning, and that was it.

♦♦♦

Dave continued, "and when things get tough, it's that mindset that pulls me through. Most things don't matter. 99% of the stuff in life doesn't matter. But, when it does matter, when it's something like cancer, you have two choices; losing, or winning. And, I wasn't okay with losing."

"Thankfully," I replied.

"Yeah, seriously," he said. "Plus, me being a winner helps other people. Winning, and helping, aren't opposites. In fact, with my goals, for me to win, requires that I help people."

"Like your charity work," I replied.

"True, but that's not what I mean. I mean like how if I lose the battle to cancer, Caren suffers. My friends suffer. If I don't win, others suffer; so you better believe I'm going to do everything I can to come out the victor."

♦♦♦

If you're anything like me, you probably want to yell at Dave and tell him that the people who love him don't look at it that way. That the people who love him don't want him to try to bear this burden all on his own. I know, I'm with you, but I've got good news. As much as he comes off that way, he knows, and he's letting others help him, which is good. I think he uses it to drive hard, because it works. And I'm certainly not going to be the one to take away his motivation. If it works, and it keeps him alive, I'm all for it.

He knows nobody feels that way, but he uses it to drive himself, so I say have at it. Bear that burden my friend, bear that burden.

♦♦♦

Dave continued, "I've faced the demon of pending death, and you know what happened? I sat down, looked at life, and asked myself the questions that matter. If I die in a year, how am I going to spend that time? What actually matters? And I found answers. I found that wealth is really the ability to wake up, and just read; not having to rush to a meeting right away. It's taking two hours in the morning seeing my wife, playing with my dog, looking at my lawn like an old man. Wealth is the fact that not only does my wife make me breakfast every day, but I can appreciate it, and show my appreciation for it. By the way, it's one of my favorite things in life, and it costs practically nothing. I've learned to ignore the fanciness, and enjoy the people. It took the threat of death for me to realize the joy of life, and I'll tell you, it's glorious."

I smiled at my friend. I must say, seeing him appreciative

of the little things was a wonderful sight.

"Make sure that's all in there," he said. "People need to know that success is about being rich in all areas that matter, not necessarily your total bank balance or how many friends you have. They need to know that if they follow the rules, they can literally have anything they want in life. They can be and do everything. They can be rich, they can be healthy, they can be free, and more importantly, they can be happy. Make sure they get all this. They need to know that in the end, as much as it doesn't seem like it, the truth is, can't doesn't exist."

Some last words...

The previous page was the ending of the original manuscript. It was mid-August when that was written, and, as you know, everything has changed, yet, nothing has changed.

I know, that seems like a contradiction, and in one way it is, but in the way that it matters, it isn't. Let me explain.

Dave's life is in the air right now. We don't know what's going to happen, and we are simply praying our hearts out, and fighting with every tool we have. Six months from now, Dave and I might be hanging out, smiling and laughing, or he might be dead. We simply don't know.

One month ago, we were confident in Dave's future. We weren't unaware of the diagnosis, but we were confident none-the-less. If there's anything that has changed, it's not our confidence that David will win, but our question of how he will win. And I don't mean how he will survive, particularly because that's still in question. What I am talking about, is only how he will win.

The part that hasn't changed, is that David is living, while he can. He is still fighting, still training, still living. The man doesn't plan on dying until his heart stops beating. Sure, he's at a low point in the story. Yes, he's not 'standing on the podium' and getting the accolades, but that's not what the winning mindset is about. It's really about trying your best. It's about giving it your all, until you've exhausted everything you can do. And because of that, Dave is still winning. Because he's fighting not for the sake of 'not dying', but to live while he can, he's winning.

In six months, if Dave's dead, he'll still have won. He'll still have lived every second he could live. And in doing that, he wins.

In late September or early October, when this book is first published, David Prentice will likely still be alive. How long after that, well, that will be up to God. Hopefully, if you are reading this book ten years after the first release, David will still be here, fighting.

If you take anything from this book, take this. Life is short, and precious. Spend time loving people. Our world, as it is, it's not going to be perfect, so don't seek perfection, just seek the good. Don't let your desire for anything overcome your desire for the good. And, Dave would punch me if I didn't include this…

Right now, change your life for the better. Don't wait.

— — — —

Now, I have a favor to ask of you. Dave's wish is to help people. If the doctors are right, and God says it isn't time for a miracle, then as you read this, Dave is likely either in his last days on Earth, or off to meet his maker.

If this book has blessed you, and you've taken up Dave on any of his challenges, please let us know by telling the world about it through whatever social media platforms you prefer, using the hashtag #watchdavewin. I cannot explain what a blessing you would be to Dave in doing so, and I thank you in advance.

If this book has benefited you, please consider buying a copy for a friend or loved who you think it could help. David Prentice changed my life, and if you do this for someone else, you may just change theirs.

— — — —

One last thing (from Josh specifically),

This isn't the right way to do things, but this is how you do things when publishing dates get moved up with almost no notice!

If you want to be kept up to date on what is going on with Dave, you can do so by joining our email list at the link below.

The link is to join the "Reader's Club" at Providingreason.com (my personal author website). While the plan was to have a separate website and email created for the book, we ran out of time, so for right now, this is how we have to do things. If you join, you will receive updates about Dave, how he's doing, and, God willing, if he's able to once again, things like speaking engagements and events. You will not be spammed, nor will your email be sold to any third parties, and there will always be an unsubscribe link at the bottom of every email should you wish to no longer receive updates. Once you sign up, you will receive a confirmation email that may get sent to your trash/junk folder in your email, so make sure to check that and confirm that it isn't junk (or it will not add you to the list). After you confirm your email, you will automatically be emailed a link to download the first 35 pages of a fiction book I wrote titled "The Road Most Taken". If you are a fiction fan, and love a good coming of age story, have a look. If not, just ignore it.

http://providingreason.com/signup/